The Six-Figure
Second Income

The Six-Figure Second Income

How to Start and Grow a Successful Online Business Without Quitting Your Day Job

DAVID LINDAHL

JONATHAN ROZEK

WILEY

John Wiley & Sons, Inc.

Published by John Wiley & Sons, Inc., Hoboken, New Jersey.
Published simultaneously in Canada.

For general information on our other products and services or for technical support, please contact our Customer Care Department within the United States at (800) 762-2974, outside the United States at (317) 572-3993 or fax (317) 572-4002.

Wiley also publishes its books in a variety of electronic formats. Some content that appears in print may not be available in electronic books. For more information about Wiley products, visit our web site at www.wiley.com.

Library of Congress Cataloging-in-Publication Data:

Lindahl, David and Rozek, Jonathan.
  The six-figure second income: how to start and grow a successful online business without quitting your day job / David Lindahl, Jonathan Rozek.
     p. cm.
  Includes index.
  ISBN 978-0-470-63395-3 (cloth)
  ISBN 978-0-470-77045-0 (ebk)
  ISBN 978-0-470-87200-0 (ebk)
  ISBN 978-0-470-87201-7 (ebk)
  1. Electronic commerce.   2. New business enterprises–Computer networks.
  I. Rozek, Jonathan, 1958- II. Title.
  HF5548.32.L556 2010
  658.8'72—dc22   2010007795

Printed in the United States of America

10 9 8 7 6 5 4 3 2 1

CONTENTS

CHAPTER 6
How to Turn Prospects into Buyers 185

Two guys wrote this book—David Lindahl and Jonathan Rozek—and we intentionally wrote the book as if it were a conversation between two people, one of whom is you.

You'll see that we say things such as, "I hope you see the value in . . ." and not "We hope you see the value in . . ." This is a more conversational and direct approach than if you constantly saw alternating versions of: "We think . . . ," "Dave says . . . ," "Jon built a . . . ," and so on.

You'll also soon see that the real secret to your six-figure second income is not in tangible products and not in gimmicks, but in honest and direct communication between you and your customers. This book is our attempt to do the same with you.

CHAPTER 1

You CAN Get Rich—But Yes, There Is a Catch

This book is about how you can make a very substantial income—a full-time income—by spending only bits and pieces of your time on the side.

You don't need to take any leaps of faith and quit your day job, nor do you need to sign up for any membership clubs or multilevel-marketing schemes. You simply can follow my tested-and-proven advice and take one baby-step after the next until you arrive at your financial destination.

If that sounds too good to be true, you're right. There is indeed a catch, and it's a big one: To be successful in building an online business, you must ignore a lot of conventional wisdom and advice. Whether it's rattling around in your head or someone's telling it to you, most of it is a combination of lies, half-truths, myths, and just plain outdated information on what it takes to be successful online.

Before I depress you too much, you should thank your lucky stars for all the garbage information published about building a business. It keeps down the real competition and means more money in your pocket if you ignore it.

Some of this bogus advice is generated by your own brain in the form of beliefs or self-doubts you've had for years. Other times you'll get the advice from well-meaning friends and family members.

Either way, it's toxic. It's my first task to clear your head of these beliefs so we can go make a bunch of money.

Let's consider these bits of bogus advice to be big *Keep Out!* signs on your way to wealth.

10 GIANT *KEEP OUT!* SIGNS ON THE ROAD TO YOUR ONLINE BUSINESS SUCCESS— THE FALSE BARRIERS

 "I'm Too Old/I'm Too Young"

Buyers on the web don't care how old or young you are— they only care what you can do for them. That might be a selfish reality, but it works in your favor. In fact, my (Jon's) son, Tom, created his first info product when he was 14 years old. He's sold it across America for years and no one has ever asked his age. It's just not relevant.

The web is the ultimate merit-based marketplace: If you have what they want, they'll buy it.

 "I Don't Have Enough Money"

Forget about the consultants who want to whack you thousands of dollars for a web site, and forget about monthly *hosting fees* of $70 or more. The truth is that you can literally be up and running with a full-featured web site for well under $100. In fact, you can have a decent one for about $50 or even less. I'll explain exactly how in this book.

Oh, and if you think you need a bunch of money to design and manufacture a product, it just isn't so. I'll show you how to create a product for next to no money and for just a little bit of your time, believe it or not.

"I Don't Have Enough Time"

You don't need big blocks of time to get a six-figure second income. All you need is scraps of time here and there.

It used to be that if you wanted a second income, you needed to go out and get a second job. That meant coming home from your first job dead tired, then wolfing down your dinner and going back out to work some more hours. Hey, you can still do that today if you want to—but it's just not necessary.

Imagine back to when the telephone was a revolutionary new device and how a conversation might have gone between someone who knew about the new technology and someone who had no clue:

> "Son, ain't no way I can leave the farm and go visit Uncle Milton in the city. This is harvest time and I have crops to get in."
>
> "But, Dad, you can go next door to the Smith's and use their new telephone."
>
> "Their what?"
>
> "Their *telephone*. You can call Uncle Milton and he'll hear your voice, plus you can hear his voice too."
>
> "But how can that be? Is it the work of the devil?"
>
> "No, Dad, it's not magic or witchcraft. It just has to do with that electricity stuff and some scientists who figured out a new way to send sounds back and forth."
>
> "Oh, I don't know. We've gotten this far without it. I see no reason to change now. . . ."

Just as it must have been hard for people to accept a revolutionary change in communication with the telephone, we're in the midst of another revolution: No longer must you spend hours each day at a second job to make the income of a second job.

This is good news and bad news, depending on the person. Some people need the structure of a job where they show up and do what they're told for several hours each day. They're okay with trading their hours for dollars.

Other people can get things done on their own without being told what to do and when to do it. Are you one of these people? I hope so, because that's the kind of person who does well with turning scraps of time into piles of money. The real trick is to know your very next step to take and to take small actions regularly. In this book, I'll supply the *what actions to take* part. You'll need to be the one to take those regular steps.

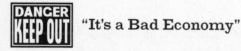 **"It's a Bad Economy"**

Let's examine that statement a little more closely. It's true that newspapers, television, and the Internet are full of bad-news stories every day. That doesn't make it a uniformly bad economy.

General Motors lays off workers in Michigan while a wind-energy company adds jobs in Texas, but let's say there is an overall 10 percent unemployment rate and another 10 percent who've given up looking. That still leaves 80 percent employment and those people are still buyers.

I'm not trying to put a pretty face on a difficult economy, but instead to make the point that there are countless *microeconomies*. If you sell custom motorcycle jackets, custom quilt designs, or a report on bass-fishing secrets, some people out there are ready-and-willing buyers right now. It's a matter of finding them, and I'll explain exactly how to do that.

 ### "All the Really Good Ideas Are Taken"

That's just crazy. Anyone who says that is starting to sound like the Roman Governor Julius Sextus Frontinus in around AD 60, who said: "Inventions have long since reached their limit, and I see no hope for further developments."

If anything, we're living in a society where the pace of new good ideas is getting quicker, not slower.

But just for argument's sake let's say that someone waved a wand and there were no additional significant inventions. Look around you—most people are collectors of things. They don't buy just one book but lots of them. They don't have one cat but several. They don't stop with one screwdriver, casserole recipe, or dog leash, but they own many.

It gets even better: As you know, people can be very passionate about hobbies. If you're a major fan of orchids, fly fishing, Jack Russell Terriers, or whatever, then you're not only a willing buyer of the next item, but you actively search for it. You want to be the first in your group to have it to show off. We'll explore this type of product in much more detail later.

"I'm Too Small to Compete Against the Big Guys"

That's early 1900s thinking, but we're in the twenty-first century now. It's true that if you wanted to compete effectively against Henry Ford back in the day, you had to be another giant like General Motors or Chrysler.

That was because you had to spend major money to set up factories, hire thousands of workers, and create dealerships around the country. It was the same for many decades in other industries: We made do with three television channels, a couple of newspapers in any given market, and the only decaffeinated coffee was *Sanka*.

These days *small* is the *new big*. I've lost count of how many hundreds of television channels are out there, not to mention all the shows on YouTube, Hulu, and so on. Newspapers are either drying up altogether or moving to 24/7 Internet access.

Everywhere you look, the old model of big, slow, and *one-size-fits-all*, is giving way to fast, agile, and *just-the-way-you-want-it*. This is wonderful news for the micromanufacturer and micromarketer you'll become after reading this book.

 "I'm No Good with Computers"

Can you turn on your computer and use a mouse? Can you read plain text on the screen? Okay then, you're good to go.

Back in the day when Bill Gates was a student fiddling with software, you needed to learn programming to make computers do anything useful. Today you no longer need to know *any* programming to get a perfectly fine web site up and running. You do need to be clear and direct in what you offer people, and that's easy to accomplish, as you'll soon discover.

 "There's Too Much Competition"

Do you want to start a business so somebody will erect a statue to you or so you can have a fat bank account? If you want the statue then by all means become a pioneer. You can tell the pioneers because they're the ones lying face-down in the mud with all the arrows in their backs. Forget that. It's much less painful and much more profitable to have your business in an area that's already somewhat established.

Consider what it's like to enter a completely new market—no visible demand exists for that product. When the first person invented crossword puzzles, computer games, and, for that matter, even the computers themselves, no immediate demand existed for them. Ken Olsen, who founded Digital Equipment Corp, said, "There is no reason for any individual to have a computer in his home."*

Demand had to be built for all these inventions. On the other hand, when you offer a new-and-improved dog collar to the market today, you have millions of potentially immediate users, depending on how good your doggie collar is.

Here's the really excellent news: Most of your competition is not very good at selling dog collars. Just think back to your own experiences in stores and through mail order. Are you consistently blown away by the excellent service you receive? At least not on Planet Earth. I'm not telling you anything new when I say that most businesses do a bland-to-terrible job of customer service. They make the really good companies stand out, and that's the kind of business I'll help you to create from scratch.

Really savvy marketers have a rule: *For fastest revenue growth, look for businesses with an existing, installed base of customers.* It's smart advice.

---

*http://www.snopes.com/quotes/kenolsen.asp

"I'm Not Educated Enough"

You definitely should sweat this one—that is, if you're applying to law school or medical school. You'll need to show some pretty impressive grades, plus don't forget those extracurricular activities and some great letters of recommendation.

Oh, you're not applying to graduate school? You just want to make money on the web? Then what does your education—or lack thereof—have to do with it? Since when did you find a great product or service online only to say to yourself: *Well it is exactly what I was looking for, but I just don't see a strong enough résumé for the inventor, so never mind.*

The plain truth is that, on the web, nobody cares about your background. That might be a disappointment if you labored for years to get a fancy degree. But it should be encouraging if you never got all the *sheepskin* you wanted. *(Note from Jon Rozek: I graduated from Harvard College with High Honors and the corporate world did care about that fact, but the Internet world and my clients could not care less and rarely even ask.)*

 "Someone Will Steal My Idea"

This one stops a lot of people dead in their tracks. They think: "I have a great idea but I'm stuck—I want to market it but as soon as I tell people about it, word will get out and some giant corporation will rip off my idea. So first I have to get it patented, but that costs money and I don't know how to go about it so maybe I'll just wait and . . ."

You know how that ends—your idea molders in your brain or, worse, you see someone else beat you to the punch by getting out there and marketing the same idea you had years before.

You can't let your overactive protection instinct squash your business idea altogether. If you let that happen then it might as well be a thief breaking into your house and stealing all your business ideas—either way, you're left with nothing to show for your asset.

It's much better to launch your product—even if it's not perfect—and start to make money with it. Pop Quiz: Who was the first person to cross the Atlantic nonstop by airplane? If you answered Charles Lindbergh, that's good. Now, who was the second person?

If you know the answer to that—without looking it up—then you really do deserve congratulations. (It's often credited to Amelia Earhart.)

If you get your product out there first, you'll be remembered as the Charles Lindbergh of that product. You won't have to sweat who else comes out with one—you'll always be able to tout yours as The Original and make fun of the imitators.

Besides, Ray Kroc, Chairman of McDonald's, was asked about all the other burger chains that sprang up after McDonald's became popular. He said, "We can invent faster than they can steal."

I bet you know people who believe some of these 10 mistaken notions. You might even be one of them. Do you see how powerful it will be when this book shows you how to navigate past these false barriers but your competition is stuck with them?

That's why I say you should thank your lucky stars for all the half-truths, myths, and bad information surrounding online businesses.

NOW FOR THE SIX DISABLING AND VERY REAL DANGERS TO YOUR ONLINE BUSINESS SUCCESS

Busting the myths was the good news, but I do have some bad news for you now. It's the stuff you really should concern yourself with—the true barriers to your progress. Let's look at each of these powerful threats to your online success.

 Real Danger Number One: You Are Easily Influenced by People Less Successful than You Want to Be

We all have people around us who mean well with their advice, but in reality they're not that helpful and not that successful themselves. It's very dangerous for you to take advice from them.

For purposes of this book, I want to put a name on this type of person. Let's call him *Uncle Moe*. For as long as you've known him, Uncle Moe has been an authority figure. He's frequently wrong but absolutely never in doubt.

He's also quite hard to ignore because he doesn't wait to be asked his opinion but instead freely volunteers it at every opportunity. Besides, Uncle Moe has in fact lived much longer than you have and he does seem to want the best for you.

Uncle Moe's opinions are not shades of gray but pure black-and-white. He either is 100 percent in favor of what you're doing or 100 percent against it.

Something's troubled you about his advice over the years—it's that frankly Uncle Moe hasn't been all that successful himself.

You've heard all of the reasons: He's had a bad back ever since the war or maybe it was also that workplace injury.

Uncle Moe never finished school because the kids came on the scene a bit earlier than he and the little lady had planned. And he's never really quite had much success in business, but it wasn't for lack of trying, he assures you.

In fact, it seems that Uncle Moe either has been in just about every type of business, or he knows someone who has. He didn't make money at real estate because "the whole industry's a scam." He almost lost his shirt in that restaurant he opened because "employees are thieves."

He tried a mail-order business once but that didn't work out because "direct mail doesn't work." He even considered going back for additional training but soon gave up that idea because "it was all that theoretical ivory-tower stuff and I've learned everything I know from the only school that counts—the School of Hard Knocks."

It's therefore hardly a surprise when you're standing over the onion dip at Thanksgiving and Uncle Moe asks you what you've been up to. You tell him that you have this idea for a new type of (whatever it is). Uncle Moe's verdict is too swift for him even to swallow, so with cheeks full of chips and dip he shakes his head: "Big mistake. I tried an even better idea a couple of years ago and couldn't get it to work. Don't waste your time."

Here's the bottom line: If Uncle Moe is highly successful then pay more attention to what he tells you. The less successful he is, the more you should politely nod and ignore his advice. Better yet, when he asks what you're up to, say something neutral like "oh, nothing special" or instead switch the topic to sports, the weather, or how his back is feeling.

You should consider a new idea of yours to be like a seedling in your garden. It's delicate, easily squashed, and needs time and nourishment in order to grow strong. Don't let the Uncle Moes of the world weed-whack your tiny plant into oblivion.

You're much better off by either keeping it to yourself or by getting advice from someone who knows about the thing you're involved with.

 Real Danger Number Two: You Think You Can Sit on the Couch and Money Will Spew out of the TV

I know what you're thinking here: That's absurd. I don't think I can sit on the couch and make money!

Here's the problem. We're all exposed to a great deal of advertising that makes things sound effortless. You can't go a day without hearing about how you can "Lose 50 pounds without dieting!" or by simply joining a dating service you can "Have that person of your dreams!"

The rational part of our brains knows that improvements and success take time, but the caveman part of our brains is sick of waiting! If someone promises instant results, hey, who knows—maybe this time it will be true.

After all, in a world where we can have instant breakfast drinks, instant messaging, and even get Dominos Pizza ordered through your television and delivered to your door, why can't long-lasting success also be delivered instantly?

One guy I know says that his goal is to make people feel like "the moment they sign up for my three-day boot camp, money will rain down on them from the sky." In other words, they don't even have to attend the event, much less put his methods into practice afterward. His goal is to make them feel like the mere act of buying his stuff will cause money to pour into their lives.

It's really a shame that nothing works that way despite the slick brochures and teleseminars to the contrary, so suppress that internal caveman when he gets all hot and heavy after hearing such talk.

Related Real Danger Number Three:
You Think that the Only Good Money Is
Hard-Earned Money

This is the flipside of what we just covered and it often gets embedded into our nervous systems from a very early age.

Google lists 4.5 million results for *U.S. Constitution,* but it shows 13.5 million results for *hard-earned money*.

There's no question that many people work extremely hard for their money. The mental limitation comes when they think that only through hard work can they produce honest money. It seems that some people apply moral overtones and believe that *easy money* is only what thieves can get away with.

What you'll discover in this book is something in between. It won't be along the lines of those fake claims like: *When you buy my system, money will spew into your life like an out-of-control ATM!* No, in fact, you'll have to do some work using only bits of time here and there. It might even involve turning off a rerun on TV in order to get something finished.

On the other hand, there won't be anything hard about it. The process is step-by-step with absolutely no leaps involved. Even better, the process involves building something once and getting paid over and over.

Think about the typical heart surgeon. She went to school for a jillion years to become trained and yes she does make a very nice income. But if she doesn't show up at the hospital to perform the next triple bypass, she doesn't get paid.

That's another way of saying the doc does *piecework*. It's much more glamorous to be a heart surgeon than to be a seamstress who must report to work and sew a thousand boxer shorts to get paid a few bucks—but both occupations are piecework. The same is true for $500-per-hour attorneys and even sports stars who get paid ridiculous sums. You don't show up to work? You don't get paid.

Compare that to making an information product one time and selling it for years or even decades afterward. Oh, you should update the information from time to time, but fundamentally you have done the work once and now will receive an income stream for a very long time.

Is that *hard-earned money*? Well, you did have to get off the couch to buy this book and you are in fact spending time to learn how to make a six-figure income on the side, so I applaud you for taking action. However, the great news is that, once you get your income vehicle moving, you can hop on and enjoy the momentum as it carries you along with relatively little effort.

I just hope you don't have some moral or religious aversion to making money without shedding any blood, sweat, or tears.

 Real Danger Number Four: You Insist upon Staying in Your Comfort Zone at All Times

It's simply not necessary to take great risks or step way outside of your comfort zone in order to make a lot of money, but stretching that zone is a good thing.

In the world of real estate investing, some so-called experts advise you to come home from work, wolf down some dinner, then change clothes and drag yourself back out, knocking on door after door to find a real estate deal. That may work from time to time, but it's just unnecessary punishment. It's also a great prescription for burnout.

I've made many millions of dollars in real estate and have never found it necessary to knock on door after door. Instead I use direct mail. I created a series of letters and figured out where to get good-quality lists of motivated sellers of real estate. Then I created a system where I brought those names to a lady at a nearby senior center, and she would address the envelopes and mail them.

It would have been more comfy for me to sit on the couch and dream about being rich someday. Instead, I had to write those letters and improve them over time. I also went through a few little old ladies to find one who did the best job for me. Those steps did not represent massive discomfort but just stretched my comfort zone a bit.

This is not a book about real estate investing, but the same principles apply to any other business. You probably know that a stretched and limber muscle performs better in running and other sports. Well, a stretched and limber brain will make you more money.

Real Danger Number Five: You Think "My Situation Is Different"

This is an extremely dangerous one. Your mom probably cradled you and told you how unique in the whole world you are. Your spouse probably has said something a tiny bit less comforting, along the lines of, "They sure broke the mold after making you!" And it's a fact that your fingerprints are unique and so is the sum of your life experiences. So far so good.

The problem comes when you use the *I'm different* concept as a shield to repel anything you don't want to hear or do.

You see a weight-loss ad and a quiet voice in your head whispers one of any number of excuses:

- She's way younger than I am—it's no wonder her body can burn off fat when mine can't.
- It's easy for an office worker to lose more weight because there's no refrigerator full of food. I'm home and it's just too tempting to open the fridge and grab something.
- It's easy for a person at home to lose more weight than I can because if you're always at home you can dictate what's in the fridge. At the office we constantly are going out to eat or having birthday cakes and so forth. I don't want to appear rude or weird so I just go with the flow and eat it, too.

That same highly skilled force-field in most people's brains can do similar repelling with any other topic—take the very book you're holding, for example.

- I could never learn to make a good second income—every other moneymaking thing I've tried has never worked.
- It's easy for native English speakers to do this stuff, but I was born in Europe and I'll always be at a disadvantage when writing things in English.
- This stuff probably worked back in 1999 when the economy was going great, but haven't you heard—we're in a real bad economy right now.
- I don't even have enough time to get a good night's sleep. And now I'm supposed to take on something else? There are only 24 hours in the day, you know, and mine are all spoken for.

The list is endless because most people have highly developed excuse generators that look like Bruce Lee in one of those martial arts movies in which he can fight off a couple dozen attackers and not even break a sweat.

I want to state clearly and for the record that your mom was right—you are unique in the world. Your spouse is also no doubt right that they're not making any more people quite like you. I'll also say right up front that I'm sure you do have plenty of challenges of one sort or another.

Given all that, here's what I'd like you to do: Instead of looking for reasons why something *won't work*, look for ways you might adapt something *to work*. Look at each interesting idea or success you hear about as a potential foothold. It might only be something you can jamb your foot into with some effort, but you will now be a step higher than you were before.

It's also how great inventions happen. A scientist let rubber cook too long by mistake and found that it became extremely hard. Rather than throw it out, he thought: *What might this stuff be useful for?* It turns out he stumbled on the process to *vulcanize* rubber, which became strong enough to make tires out of.

Another scientist worked for the 3M Company and found a particularly useless type of glue. It wasn't strong at all. He fiddled around with what it might be useful for and discovered that, if he painted some of it on the back of paper, it would stick to things but could easily be removed. He tried it on notations to his music while playing in an orchestra and it was just the thing. The *Post-it Note* was born.

Maybe you have a great invention inside of you too, but that's not my point. I only want you to recognize your mental Bruce Lee every time he gets ready to karate-chop another opportunity. Tell him instead to hit the showers while you think if there's anything useable in the idea.

Even this instant I bet your Bruce Lee is working against you: "*Well, the next time I invent glue or I am a scientist in a rubber lab, I'll be sure to keep my eyes open. But I'm just a (whatever you are). Nothing exciting happens to me so my situation's different."*

No, it's not. In Chapter 2, which is about developing a product, I'll give you lots of ideas on how to get a product to sell. Right now all I want is for you to begin to recognize that decidedly unhelpful voice in your brain and stick it off in a corner when it pipes up.

 Real Danger Number 6: You're More of an Idea Pack Rat than a Beaver

Pack rats are famous for lining their nests with shiny objects like buttons, tinsel, foil, and wire. The human equivalent is someone who is forever looking for the next *Big Deal*.

Here again, marketers are more than happy to oblige. A few years ago they proclaimed, "The Internet is dead—here comes the SuperNet!" Then it was, "Direct mail is dead—now it's all about e-mail marketing!" A short time later we all were treated to yet another proclamation: "E-mail is dead—now it's all about blogs!" Then they heralded Facebook as the next big thing—until someone else swore the real game-changer was Twitter.

These are often the same hucksters who told you that you could sit on the couch and money would spew from the TV. They want to be the pioneer whom you pay for the silver bullet that you seek to solve all your problems in one fell swoop.

It ain't gonna happen. Occasionally someone will figure out a clever angle and make some money from it. Then—just like the California Gold Rush—as soon as word gets out, there's a mad scramble to get in on the action. Prices go up and the quality of the opportunity plummets.

That story should only be depressing for the human pack rat, because the good news is that plenty of methods still work just fine for making money online. No single method is revolutionary, just as nothing is the single super-food you probably want to eat for the rest of your life to the exclusion of all else.

It's much better to style yourself after the beaver. After a bit of planning it decides that a certain spot will become its home. Then it doesn't look for the single, absolutely perfect monster tree to make a dam with. Instead it looks for branches and limbs it can conveniently find, fashioning each one to fit.

At first the dam isn't much to look at, but with steady effort it begins to work. Once the beaver dam is built the main effort is done and now only a bit of maintenance is needed to keep things working.

By all means keep your eyes open for the next technology that can make your life easier—whatever that might be. Then, instead of dumping everything else in favor of that shiny object, simply look for how it might fit into what you already have in place in that money-dam of yours.

Whew! We've succeeded in busting through lots of false barriers to your success and then making sure you're aware of the biggest real dangers to that second income we're about to build for you.

Can you see why this opportunity is not *too good to be true*? It takes some effort to ignore the false barriers and avoid the real dangers. I'll say it again: All these barriers and dangers are great for you because they mean less competition.

I hope you had your pen out and have underlined the sections of this chapter that had particular relevance to you, because I suggest you review those sections regularly.

It's so easy to be lulled back into thinking in those old, counterproductive ways.

The next chapter is the opposite of counterproductive— I'm going to turn you into a product machine so that you see opportunity and potential profits just about everywhere you look.

CHAPTER 2

How to Build a Quick and Profitable Product

Did you get a chance to watch the TV show *Pitchmen* on The Discovery Channel before it was cancelled? If not, maybe you can find episodes on the Internet. I suggest you watch a few shows because it will make you feel so very good about what you're about to discover in the book you're holding.

The show starred two long-time marketers or *pitchmen*, Billy Mays and Anthony "Sully" Sullivan. (The show was canceled after Billy unexpectedly died.) You probably have seen Billy pitch stuff like cleaners and gadgets on television for years. He was very entertaining and sold a ton.

Though the show was entertaining, it was also sad in a way. Here's how a typical segment of the show worked:

An inventor whom we'll call Gus worked for years designing a new-and-improved gizmo like a cup holder for the car or perhaps a pocket fishing rod. He sank his life-savings into designing the product and having it manufactured. Now pallet after pallet of them sits in a warehouse. It seems that his own version of Uncle Moe had plenty of advice on how to sell them but nothing worked.

Through hit and miss, Gus became aware of the *Pitchmen* show and he wrangled an appointment. He got to stand at one end of a conference table while he demonstrated his cup holder to Billy and Sully for perhaps 60 seconds. The guys asked two or three questions and formulated an instant impression of the product.

In the vast majority of cases both Billy and Sully looked at each other—then, as politely as they could, they thanked Gus for his interesting product and ushered him out of the room. Another inventor's dreams dashed. In a handful of cases Billy and Sully took on the new product and cut a deal where they financed the next phase in exchange for a very healthy cut of the profits.

The next phase involved making sure the product didn't infringe on someone else's trademark or patent, and they reviewed how easily and cheaply it could be mass-produced. Finally, they made a test commercial and ran it in several markets.

The cost of this next phase was always in the five figures and sometimes into six figures. Judging from comments on the show only a fraction of those product candidates ever broke even, never mind making a substantial profit.

I found the process sad because the odds were so stacked against these people making it to the Big Time. They usually mortgaged their houses and sank their life-savings into the project, in most cases only to be rejected by Billy and Sully.

Even when they made it to the final test round, their chances of breaking even were slim and the chances of realizing their dreams and making a fortune seemed to be about as likely as winning the lottery.

In my opinion, that's no way to build a second income. You're betting too much money and time against too many factors that are way out of your control. Let's look at all the bad things about this approach:

- You toil for years to perfect your product in secret with no income to show for it.
- You must spend more money to try to protect your idea through patents, nondisclosure agreements, memorandums of understanding, and contracts, while your lawyer's billing clock spins and spins.

- You must pray that you know someone who knows someone who can get you an introduction to someone.
- Then you must pray that your 60-second presentation goes well.
- When it most likely does not go well, you lick your wounds. If the honchos like your product you gulp as you sign away most of your future profits.
- Now you pray some more that the product does well.

Look, if you're a hobbyist/tinkerer and just enjoy making gadgets, then more power to you. Obviously a few people do get their inventions to market from time to time and maybe even make a nice profit from them.

My point is that, if you're going down that route, do it for the excitement of the unknown or for the miniscule chance that you'll be on television someday. Don't do it because you think that's the only way to make money from selling a product.

THE TYPICAL DREAM IS USELESS

We met Uncle Moe in the last chapter. He has an ego even bigger than his beer belly and is a know-it-all when it comes to your life and everyone else's. Moe likes you and tells you that this whole idea of selling stuff is for the birds. He's tried it and it simply won't work.

Believe it or not, in one sense I agree with Uncle Moe. That's because the typical dream of making it big is so extremely unrealistic, as people pitching the Pitchmen usually discovered. Here are the underlying requirements that make this conventional approach so very difficult to pull off:

1. I must have a fortress to protect my idea from knock-off artists.

2. I must reach millions of people.
3. I want to be famous.
4. I want to be as rich as King Midas from this first invention of mine.
5. I need to invent something revolutionary.
6. Inventions are things that are manufactured in factories.

I would agree with Uncle Moe that you, or I, or anyone else are exceedingly unlikely to meet all six requirements in a lifetime.

Fortunately, a far superior method exists for building a substantial income. Let's look at each of those requirements and replace it with something better:

"I Must Have a Fortress to Protect My Idea from Knockoff Artists"

Unless you want to pay for an army of lawyers, it's unrealistic to expect effective protection. Even if you prevailed in the United States, what are you going to do about Asian countries where intellectual-property piracy has been rampant, despite even U.S. government actions? You're much better off remembering the quote in the last chapter about what McDonald's chairman Ray Kroc said: "We can invent faster than they can steal."

Did I just hear you think to yourself, *"My situation's different and I don't have the resources of Ray Kroc"*? That wasn't you? Oh good. That must have been someone else thinking that, because you now know better. Besides, even if you didn't invent faster than the thieves could knock you off, you could always claim to be the *genuine article*, the *first-ever*, and urge customers to *accept no substitutes*.

"I Must Reach Millions of People"

No, Proctor and Gamble must reach millions of people for a new toothpaste to be profitable. You only need to find hundreds or perhaps a few thousand people worldwide for your product to make you a very nice pile of dough, as you'll soon see.

"I Want to Be Famous"

Okay, if that's what you're after, I can't argue with that. But you can work up to being famous, can't you? First, make a bunch of money with a product and then you'll have plenty of resources to go after fame.

"I Want to Be as Rich as King Midas from the First Invention of Mine"

Again, think more about the trajectory you're on than the ultimate destination. You're setting yourself up for failure if every time you are at bat in a baseball game, you must uncork a grand slam or you regard it as a failure. Even the mighty Mississippi River starts as a few trickles and then combines over time to become something impressive.

"I Need to Invent Something Revolutionary"

No, you don't. Think back to your last 10 purchases. How many of them are one-of-a-kind revolutionary, versus products you just liked? If you bought light bulbs, then yes the invention of the light bulb was revolutionary, but you bought *Acme brand* because they were a good value. Acme got your business even though dozens of other companies make light bulbs. It's the same with coffee, computers, cars, and almost all other products. You can make a bundle of money by carving out your corner of an existing product category.

"Inventions Are Things that Are Manufactured in Factories"

Of course it's true that some inventions fit that description, but it doesn't mean yours has to be one of them. When I think of factories, all I see are employees, buildings, rules, regulations, red tape, headaches, and big expenses.

Similar to the fame discussion above, let's start small, nimble, and cheap, and, after you have a pile of money in front of you, only then think about building that giant plant with your name over the door.

We've just talked about the classic, slow, painful, and costly way of making money with a product. Now let's talk about the superior way.

YOUR FIRST PRODUCT SHOULD BE ONE OF THESE

Your first moneymaker should be an *information product*. I'm not saying that all other types of products are bad or unworkable—I'm simply focused on getting you the most money in the shortest time for the least amount of effort on your part. Here's how an information product stacks up against the classic type of product we just discussed.

You may be reading this book while you already have a physical product and just want to know how to market it more effectively. That's fine, and I'll definitely boost your marketing power in later chapters. But if you do not yet have a product, I hope you see that the choice is clear—go for the information product, or *info product* for short.

TABLE 2.1   Physical Products or Information Products:
Which sounds better to you?

CHARACTERISTIC	PHYSICAL PRODUCTS	INFORMATION PRODUCTS
Time it takes from idea to first sale	Relatively long process to design and manufacture—typically months or even years.	Relatively short process. Can be as short as days.
Ability of someone to swipe your idea	Pretty good.	Pretty good.
Ability to come out with another product quickly	Relatively difficult.	Relatively easy.
Hoops to jump through	Not bad if you like lawyers, paperwork, contracts, permits, and red-tape.	Very few hoops.
Profit margin	Maybe okay if you're a cottage industry, but slim if you try to scale to the big-time, because your investment will go way up.	Large when you start out and large as you grow.
Likelihood of a first-timer pulling it off	Relatively slim.	Relatively good.
Prestige	Great feeling of having your name on the door, but you'll pay big bucks for that honor.	No prestige to speak of, and your relatives won't understand what business you're in. They'll just know you have more money than you did before.

John Lennon, the Beatles band member, once said, "I'm going to write a swimming pool." He understood that he was in the info product business. If he sat down and wrote a single song, he could pay for a swimming pool. Now don't you go saying, "Oh, my situation's different—John Lennon was a world-famous musician." Yes, he was, and perhaps from a standing start you can only put something together that can buy a bicycle or a dinghy. So what? Lennon's first song wouldn't have earned himself a swimming pool. If he had insisted on instant mega-success, he'd have lived his life in Liverpool, England.

Let's now talk about the many types of info products you can create, and we'll do it in the context of a series of simple but extremely powerful questions.

What Problem Have You Solved?

Guys are accused of never asking for directions and never reading the owner's manual. Though that may be true, it's also true that most owner's manuals are terribly written. I bet you've been frustrated with tiny print in 16 different languages, not to mention the nonsense warnings that some attorney inserted along the lines of: "Do not operate toaster in bathtub."

People want to know the straightforward, quick, easy way to operate things. I'm not suggesting that you rewrite toaster owner's manuals, but rather that you think back to what has frustrated you in the past. Maybe you figured out a novel way to organize all your model train parts, fishing gear, or quilting supplies. If you are a big fan of some hobby, you're intimately aware of the frustrations that most fans suffer and you've maybe even solved some of them. That can make you money.

No, it's not revolutionary, and maybe only 10,000 people worldwide have that problem. Hey, if you can reach them efficiently and at low cost, might a fraction of them be so tired of the same problem that they'd be willing to pay you for an answer?

Start with what physical thing frustrates you or someone you know. If you're frustrated by *senseless violence* or *modern society*, sorry—this is the wrong book to fix that. Now think of a solution that either you have found or someone you know has found. We'll talk later about how to turn that solution into an info product.

What Can You Demonstrate?

My (Jon's) daughter, Christina, loves to do the fabric art of *tie-dye*. Though tie-dye was popular with hippies in the 1960s, even in the twenty-first century that art form has a following. If you go onto Amazon, you'll see at least one person who set up a camera in front of a table and demonstrated tie-dye techniques. The DVD costs almost $30, even though DVDs can be made for about a buck each.

Do I care that the person is making an absurdly large profit margin on this DVD? Not at all. I simply want to see how Christina might benefit from it and how good the Amazon reviews are for that product.

Now consider the maker of the DVD. He didn't even have to create a web site or buy traffic to come to it. He posted his DVD on Amazon and I went there, looking for good tie-dye stuff. Amazon will take a hunk of his profit but so what— he'll still make a percentage profit from the DVD that's better than any *Fortune 500* company could ever achieve.

What can *you* demonstrate? Is it how to sharpen lawn-mower blades? How to spin yarn made from yak fur? How to retrofit a chainsaw to run on nitrous? How to play music with the tones from your *Apple iPhone*?

Yes, sometimes even the crazy and nonutilitarian stuff like techno-tricks will sell well. Imagine guys hunched over at a bar trying to impress each other—or a girl—with the things only they know how to do with their *BlackBerry* or *iPhone*. Don't you suppose a guy would pay seven dollars for a way to impress the lady at the other end of that bar?

"But that's too little to charge for a product!" you say. I would reply that you're falling into *Uncle Moe thinking*. I agree that you might not be able to make a fortune from a seven-dollar product, but you don't need to make a fortune off something that takes you an afternoon to create. All you're aiming for is a little stream of income that over time will combine with other little streams to make your Mississippi Money River.

I know a guy who's made as much as $30,000 in one single day from a series of short reports he's written and marketed. We're talking usually fewer than 10-page reports. Sometimes he'll write one as a passenger in a car while driving to a relative's house for dinner.

I know another guy who does his best writing while watching mindless *sitcoms* on television. They relax him and he just types away at an idea on his keyboard when one floats through his brain. He's a multimillionaire now.

Maybe it would take you a week to write your first 10-pager, using bits and pieces of time. Maybe two weeks. So what?

What Have You Researched on the Web and Discovered?

One guy has made a fortune with a kidney stone remedy online. He's not a doctor, nurse, or any other kind of medical professional. Think about that for a moment. Lots of people would stop dead in their tracks and never consider writing about the kidney stone treatment they stumbled upon. They'd think, *"Oh I'm not a doctor so who would listen to me about kidney stones?"*

Let me tell you—as someone who's had them (Jon), kidney stone sufferers are highly motivated to look for remedies. Besides, some of the doctor remedies involve surgery, nasty drugs, and some very bad side effects. If someone discloses up front that he's not a doctor but he's collected a series of possible folk remedies that involve stuff as harmless as asparagus and watermelons—you can bet I'll try his stuff in a *New York minute*.

It's important not to pretend to be something you're not. Otherwise you'll have many refunds when people discover the truth, not to mention the Federal Trade Commission coming down on you.

But sometimes you can use the *outsider* perspective to your advantage. In the case of the kidney stone treatment, it could be "I went to the doc and nothing seemed to work. Then I started to ask my friends and found out that several of them had remedies that had been handed down for generations. . . . "

If you look in those newspaper mini-magazine inserts that come before the weekend, from time to time you'll see reports like *Hydrogen Peroxide—the Miracle Worker*, or *101 Uses for Cider Vinegar*. I doubt that those authors are chemists who toiled in the lab for years to discover many uses for vinegar or hydrogen peroxide. They probably scoured the web and talked with lots of friends.

This is a good time to discuss plagiarism—don't do it. Not only can it get you into all sorts of legal hot water, but it is also simply unnecessary to copy someone else's words to be successful. Even though I've seen the cider vinegar report, I could come out with another one and be completely safe. For instance, I'd use my own words and do a piece on *Cider Vinegar for Athletes*, which might describe a dozen uses just for them, or I might do *Top 25 uses for Apple Cider Vinegar*.

Would some of those applications be the same general nature as what was in the booklet I came across? Of course they would. But think about the so-called *original author*—we all have grandmothers who've used vinegar for generations to do things like clean windows or soothe bug bites. That original author didn't invent these uses, but simply compiled them in his or her own words.

When you free yourself from the arbitrary and unnecessary requirement to be *totally original*, think of the vast possibilities that open up in front of you! An enterprising person—you?—could sit down and make a list of all the other types of common home ingredients like lemon juice, tomato juice, salt, rubbing alcohol, baking soda, and so on. Then you could spend the time yourself—or hire relatives, kids, or senior citizens—to look far and wide for all sorts of uses.

You could then compile small paragraphs about all the uses for lemon juice, for instance. One secret would be to include many pictures. So if you're discussing insect bites, show a nasty red mosquito bite.

You could either take those pictures yourself, or simply go to one of the stock-photo agencies on the web to buy them. You don't know about *microstock agencies*, as they're known? Oh, let me digress. Here's another great example of people making money in this new economy.

The lousy old way of getting photos for your products was to hire a professional or you had to go to a big, arrogant stock-photo agency. They would charge you hundreds or even thousands of dollars for a single solitary photograph. And they wouldn't stop there—they then would require you to pay them a royalty every time that photo was published! I can see that if you took a special photo of Marilyn Monroe you might want to capitalize on it forever. But a picture of a watermelon patch? Give me a break.

Along came the Internet and some enterprising people who decided to cut out the middlemen—in other words, cut out the big arrogant agencies and photographers. Now it's no longer a monopoly but a marketplace. Tens of thousands of photographers can upload their pictures to these sites, which classify them by phrases like *watermelon*, or *people having fun*, or *frustrated*. When you go to the site and type in "frustrated," you'll see hundreds of photos of people pulling their hair out, grimacing, and so forth.

Better yet, you can buy the photos for as little as one dollar each with no continuing royalties. It's a true win-win-win—you win because you get a great picture out of many variations you reviewed; the photographer made a few pennies on the photograph; and so did the microstock agency.

Before you think this is ripping off the photographer, think again. I recently read about a graduate student at Brown University who—in his spare time between studying—makes *six figures per year* just taking photographs of things around town. He only makes pennies per photograph, but some of his pictures are bought by thousands of people, and he's uploaded thousands of photos over the course of a few years.

Isn't that incredible? You or someone in your family could do the exact same thing. This guy could have made all sorts of excuses like *I'll do the photography when I have more time after I get out of school*, or *I'm not a professional photographer, so who would buy my pictures*. Instead, he uses his spare time to make more money than do the prestigious professors who teach him.

If you want to know more about microstock agencies, simply go to www.sixfiguresecondincome.com and type in the term "photo." I have a list of the most current and best agencies I've come across. Rather than print the list in this book and run the risk of it being outdated, you'll get a current list by going to the site.

Back to my original point: Stick pleasing or descriptive pictures in your small report about lemon juice and it will sell better. People are highly visual creatures and they find documents with pictures to be more inviting.

How long does the report have to be? I've seen special reports of only two typed pages written simply in Microsoft Word—with no pictures or other formatting—and they successfully sold for 10 dollars. If the content is valuable, often the length isn't too important. There are exceptions to that rule, and we'll cover them later in this book. But remember that you're not writing for your English teacher who demanded a 10-page essay in high school. You're writing for people who don't have much time, probably don't love to read, and just want solutions quickly.

What Are the Best Resources You've Found?

A friend of mine is a successful, high-profile marketer. He made a point of being on television and in newspapers. I guess he was after that fame we discussed earlier. Anyway, one day he was home with his family and two armed men busted into his home. One stayed with his wife and kids downstairs while the other ordered my friend upstairs to clean out the jewelry and other valuables.

It turned out they were messing with the wrong guy, because my friend is a world-ranked expert in martial arts. He disarmed the attacker, who ran downstairs and out the door with his accomplice.

Needless to say, my friend was rattled by the experience. Rather than complain or withdraw into a shell he decided to do something about it. As you may know, tools like Google Earth make it simple to find addresses, and other tools can scour motor vehicle registries and other sources to put together files the CIA would be proud of. That's what his attackers must have done.

Now, instead of wanting a high profile, my friend wanted the money but no longer the fame. Over a period of months he was able to assemble a group of people with different talents to erase much of the publicity and contact information on the Internet about him.

Well, wouldn't you suppose that other wealthy people might want to know what my friend discovered through months of research? Now he has turned a real lemon—the home invasion—into lemonade by selling his knowledge for thousands of dollars. Here again, some readers of this book will think: *"That's nice, but I haven't been the victim of a home invasion. My situation's different, so I can't benefit from that story."* See what I mean when I said earlier that the "my situation's different" mentality is so pervasive?

You don't need to be a victim to benefit from this story. You could scour the web and put together tips that were printed in various newspapers and magazines over time. You'd put them in your own words, of course. Imagine the dramatic product you could create by going to a county jail and interviewing a few burglars about what they look for and how homeowners can protect themselves. That's been done before, but so what—it's a timeless angle and most readers would want to hear what today's burglars look for, and not the bad-guy techniques from years ago.

Besides, if you or a loved one were a victim of a crime, don't you suppose that you would become an absolutely voracious collector of all available information to prevent it from happening again? Because that sort of crime happens all over the world, you'd also have a worldwide audience of potential buyers.

How Do Things Fit Together?

There's a type of software that I would not particularly recommend, but that's called Joomla. It creates web sites for you, but before you go out and research Joomla, I'll tell you later how to get web sites created even easier.

At one point I thought Joomla would be a great tool to build sites. I quickly became frustrated because it involved a lot of nit-picky, detailed installation instructions for it to work just right.

Because I knew that Joomla was reasonably popular I figured there must be information online about how to make the installation go more smoothly. Sure enough a marketer had posted a video about it. He was a Joomla fan and simply did a *screen capture* of his screen as he buzzed through the installation process on his computer desktop while verbally describing the process. Later you'll discover exactly what software to use so you can do the same thing.

He wrote a quick web page to describe how frustrating it is to install Joomla if you don't know a handful of tricks. When I read that description I knew his video was for me. In this case he didn't even go to the bother of creating a DVD for me to buy on Amazon. Instead, he had a video I could download after paying $59.

This man spent a couple of hours recording the video and then probably three more hours creating a web page and hooking it up to a payment system. He therefore had perhaps five hours invested in this info product. I bought it without much hesitation because his video was the shortest route between where I was and having this Joomla thing figured out. Besides, he gave a solid money-back guarantee if I was not satisfied. We'll talk in much more detail later about the dos and don'ts of effective guarantees.

I was indeed able to install Joomla quickly after watching his video. With the popularity of that software it would not surprise me if he's sold hundreds of copies of that video at $59 a pop. That's thousands of dollars of pure profit from being frustrated, figuring out a solution, and then documenting the steps to that solution for others to follow.

Expand your mind to the thousands of products out there. Now everything seems to have a computer inside and manufacturers compete with each other to add lots of features. That spells confusion for many people.

An enterprising person could record a whole series of videos or audios on just Brother® sewing machines, for example. If I buy the Brother CS-6000i sewing machine I may be willing to drop another 15 bucks to have the computer console explained and demonstrated.

But here's the fantastic part: If I own any other Brother sewing machine—never mind a different brand—I'm only going to want a guide to my exact model. In this case the "my situation's different" phenomenon works in your favor as a marketer! You can create videos for each of the Brother sewing machines. Maybe a few models are way different from the rest, but I'll bet that most of them have many features in common.

After you made all the Brother videos, you could move on to each of the other sewing machine manufacturers. The news gets even better: Because you have such a specific, laser-focused product like *Video setup guide for the Brother CS-6000i Sewing Machine*, you'll shoot to the top of the Google rankings whenever someone types in "Brother CS-6000i sewing machine." You're not trying to make a one-size-fits-all type of video, but a highly specific one. Owners of that machine want highly specific answers. It's a match made in heaven and one that will compensate you well.

You may wonder: *Why wouldn't the manufacturers make these videos?* It's possible that a few of them have videos but it's also possible that they're made by sewing machine experts or engineers who live and breathe sewing machines. It's kind of like a doctor offering only a limited spectrum of harsh remedies for kidney stones.

Sometimes consumers want to hear from other consumers. They hunger for realistic commentary like—and I'm making this up—"The owner's manual for the CS-6000i will give you a long and complicated way to set the thread tension, but I've found a better way. . . ."

I've spent a while describing the easy profit potential for just sewing machine videos. Of course the same holds true for bass boat motors, bread machines, bandsaws for wood or metal, greenhouses, and countless other products. In a sense this entire book is one big guide that answers the question: "How does this whole money-making concept fit together?"

EXPLORE OTHER VARIATIONS ON A PROVEN THEME

Let's say you are expert at some topic like growing tomatoes. Of course you could come out with a guide to growing them, despite the fact that when I just typed in *growing tomatoes* in Amazon's book section, 289 results came back.

Such a statistic should not depress you into thinking: *"There's nothing I could possibly add to the topic of growing tomatoes if there are already 289 books on Amazon about them."* Instead you should conclude: *"Wow, there seems to be an inexhaustible appetite for anything relating to the growing of tomatoes!"*

Besides, you simply need to find a slight twist or variation on the topic. For instance, some of the titles relate to heirloom varieties of tomatoes. Others have to do with organic cultivation, indoor cultivation, how kids can grow them, and even how to grow them upside-down. You could sit over a beer or coffee and think of many other angles, I'm sure:

- Tomato Gardening in New England
- How to Grow a Multicolored Garden of Tomatoes
- How to Grow the Smallest Tomatoes You've Ever Seen
- Tomato Remedies for a Variety of Illnesses
- A Student's Guide to Growing Tomatoes in a Dorm Room

Are you getting the idea of how you can take a central concept and spin an unlimited number of narrow and separate products from it? It's even realistic to imagine that one person—albeit a tomato lover—could do a dozen of these info products over the course of the off-season for tomatoes and have them all for sale the following spring.

Another great set of variations would be *myths*, *pitfalls*, and *shortcuts*. People are impatient, as you know. That's why many software programs these days ship with a *quick-start guide*. In that same vein, you can think about short-cuts to getting something done. Perhaps it's how to grow tomatoes better indoors using the new LED lights so you get a jump on the outdoor growing season.

I (Dave) have been extremely successful with a special report in my real estate investing business. It's called: *23 Mistakes Real Estate Investors Make, and How To Avoid Them*. I've had thousands of people request that report. It was my first contact with those people from whom I've generated many millions of dollars in sales.

It's worth thinking hard about that angle of mistakes, pitfalls, or myths—beginners will want to read the report because they know they're starting out and want to avoid as many problems as possible. However, the same report will be tantalizing to novices and experts, too—they become curious and wonder, *"Hey, what if this guy knows a thing or two I don't . . . might that save me time and money?"*

Therefore, most people are curious enough to download and even pay for a report that helps them to avoid mistakes, pitfalls, or myths.

You know how useful some *Frequently Asked Questions* (FAQ) sections are on the web? You could even create a report that had a more comprehensive set of questions and answers. It could be: *100 Questions and Answers about Dutch Porcelain.*

What Have You Tested?

Consumer Reports made a big name for itself by running tests on all sorts of products. Still, that company can only cover a handful of products each year. What about the other millions of products and services offered each year, not to mention what's already on the market?

Recently, I was looking for a *reel push mower*. You know the kind that has a cylindrical, spiral set of blades that cut grass, rather than the flat mowers that shred the grass? Reel mowers are making a comeback because some of them have no engines, so they don't belch fumes and are in keeping with the Green Movement. Besides, they're quiet so you can mow pretty much any time of the day without disturbing anyone.

When I was researching the best one to buy, just about all the information I could find was from the manufacturers themselves. That's semi-helpful and better than nothing, especially when the manufacturers tell me factually how their mowers are the best instead of just showering me with meaningless adjectives like *revolutionary*, *user-friendly*, and *unique*.

I never did find someone who sold a $10 to $15 report that compared the five or so top-selling mowers. He could have gone to mower repair shops and asked the mechanics which mowers have the fewest repair calls. He could have interviewed a few salespeople and maybe even found owners of the various models. With a weekend of work he could have compiled a useful and valuable report that compared the mowers in terms of cost, warranty, weight, compactness, ease of use, number of blades, number of accessories, repair locations, how long the companies have been in business, sources for online videos of the products, and so on.

If I was contemplating the expenditure of $300 or so for a mower, I just might spend 10 bucks to help ensure I made the right decision.

APPEAL TO RABID HOBBYISTS

In the last chapter I talked about how most people are collectors, whether they realize it or not. There are the conventional collectors of things like bottles and fine porcelain. But other collectors are less visible, like people who collect old software, typewriters, wine labels, airline barf bags (I kid you not), anything with a dog/cat/bird/monkey on it, movie stars who collect husbands—the list is endless.

Most definitely, if you determine what you're a collector of, you can be sure there are other people with your same interest. You can go to www.meetup.com and see for yourself. The web site lists groups all over creation. In fact, it claims that the site covers 28,000 topics in 45,000 cities around the world. It's a great place to get ideas for groups you can join, or simply for people you could interview about whatever you're researching.

Here's a really great idea for you: As you know from our earlier example, there are plenty of guides on how to grow tomatoes and I encourage you to add to the vast collection.

But very few marketers tap into the concept of selling a special report to tomato enthusiasts along the lines of *How to Make Money with Your Tomato Gardening Hobby.*

Think about that for a minute. These people already are rabid collectors of anything tomato, right? Probably to the chagrin of their spouses, who think they're nuts, no doubt— that is, unless they met at a tomato convention. So what would be better than to sell them a guide about their passion in life—tomatoes—but one that explains how they can make money with their passion?

As you probably know, many people decide to buy things based upon their emotions, but they want to justify their decisions on rational grounds. For instance, a guy wants to buy a Mercedes because deep down he's always wanted one and thinks he'll look cool in it. However, he says, "Honey, just think how much safer we'll be in the Mercedes—after all that's what they drive on the German Autobahn, plus it's German-engineered, and we all know how good German products are, and . . ."

He just wants the car, but he'll list his best rational reasons for it, and he's keeping his fingers crossed that she'll buy that argument. Back to the tomato nut: He just wants anything that has to do with tomatoes. If you sell him a report that makes the rational argument that he can now make money with his hobby, passion, obsession, or whatever you call it—well, that's music to his ears.

You may ask *"But how can I tell him how to make money with tomatoes? I don't know anything about them besides how to eat one."* That's where you made a smart move to buy this book! You're learning how to turn just about anything into a moneymaking info product. The very concepts you are discovering in this chapter can be repurposed for the tomato grower. You could easily do a 10- or 20-page report all about how that person could find a topic to write about, or how she could prepare a DVD for sale on Amazon or as a video download.

That tomato grower has not read this book but you soon will have. That means you are in a position to offer a guide to that person. Then when you've cornered the market for guides on making money with tomatoes you can move to orchids, parakeets, and any of thousands of other hobbies.

I can hear you saying, *"But I have no credentials yet to be able to talk about making money by growing tomatoes or with any other such report. I better wait."* Well, you could do that, but remember the Brown University student who could have made excuses about his photographic inexperience. Instead, he took action and is now raking in the dough. Let's also consider the kidney stone guy and his report—I really could not have cared less that he was not a doctor, and I didn't even care whether he had ever suffered from kidney stones before. I only wanted access to possible remedies that were traditional, easy, and safe. I wanted to know I could get my money back if they didn't work, and that was it. I was ready to buy and I bought.

You can be in the same position with scores of simple reports as soon as you put your mind to it even briefly.

Is This Great, or What?

Now let's think about all those concerns that Uncle Moe had earlier about making money with a new product.

1. *I'll need a fortress to protect my idea:* No, you won't. It's a 10-page report on a Brother sewing machine, for Pete's sake! I don't think the Chinese government will be conspiring to knock off that report.
2. *I must reach millions of people:* Forget that. If you write a report on a Saturday and get it all set up for sale by the end of Sunday, you don't need to sell

millions or even thousands of them to make a very handsome profit.

3. *I want to be famous:* Okay, these small reports will not make you famous. Moe's right on that one. You'll just have to find some other activity that will accomplish that goal.

4. *I want to be as rich as King Midas from this first invention:* Highly unlikely that it will happen. You didn't build the Great Pyramid of Giza but spent a few hours or perhaps a few days on the project, so it's unlikely to bring you everlasting wealth and glory. It will, however, create one of those small streams that—when added to the other streams you can easily build—collectively can be as large as you'd like.

5. *I need to invent something revolutionary:* Nope. You need to invent something even just slightly different. It could be more detailed or in a different medium like video or audio, or it could appeal to a narrower but more passionate audience. That's all that is necessary.

6. *Inventions are things that are manufactured in factories:* Absolutely true in the beginning of the twentieth century, but not at the beginning of the twenty-first. We all use physical objects that are forged, mixed, or stamped, and we probably always will use them. You get to choose to make money in a new and much easier marketplace—a global and almost instant one.

ANOTHER SCHOOL OF THOUGHT

You're going to hear some marketers say there's a much better way to find a product. They'll insist that the correct way to make a bunch of money is to find a hot trend and get in front of it.

Here's how that would work. You can use two Google tools that most people have no clue about—Google Trends at www.google.com/trends and Google Insights for Search at www.google.com/insights/search. These are wonderful tools that are also free. Google Trends will tell you the hot current trends, and Google Insights for Search will tell you how long they've been hot and in what regions of the country or the world.

Again, the concept is to find something really hot and then create a product for that market. There's nothing wrong with that thinking, and, if you find something promising with those tools, by all means create a product for it.

I bring up this method after all the other ones simply because you may find it a bit more difficult to accomplish at first. I'm trying to undo decades of Uncle Moe's influence, after all. I want you to get a little stream of income just as quickly and easily as possible so you stand back, wide-eyed, and go: "Wow! This stuff really does work! I can't wait to do it over and over again!"

In my opinion, that easy, early win will best come from building an info product around something you already know well. It will involve less research and you'll already know all the jargon, myths, pitfalls, and so on.

If you're *gung-ho* to try the hot-trend angle, then please guard against early discouragement, which can be fatal to your profit plans. It may take you longer to get the product out and have it become highly visible, and you may lack the motivation to see it through.

AVOID THIS PITFALL

I know this next pitfall from personal experience so I want you to avoid it: Do not get all excited about creating a product without checking what's out there already. Don't get me wrong—I'm not saying that you need to find an untouched market. On the contrary, I just finished saying how you can make good money by doing yet another guide about growing tomatoes despite the 289 other guides out there.

What I am saying is you need to know the lay of the land before marketing your info product and preferably before even creating it. When you get a great idea it's a temptation to not search on the web for it, because you don't want to be disappointed to discover that someone else has already created a great video to the Brother CS-6000i sewing machine—though that's pretty unlikely.

Resist the temptation to stick your head in the sand. Do some solid research up front for two reasons: First, if in fact there is something *exactly* like what you were going to create, you've now saved yourself a lot of time. Second, your potential customers are searching all around for what new materials exist on a particular topic. It's to your advantage to be able to speak intelligently about your info product, as in: "This is the first guide that breaks down to easy steps the complicated process of recalibrating the Mark VI Widget. . . ."

You may remember some years ago how there was a national obsession with prescription drug prices. Congress was considering laws that would have made it legal to import Canadian prescription drugs, which at the time were far less expensive for the same medicine than were the American drugs.

I did some initial research on the topic and realized there seemed to be a huge opportunity to fill a gaping hole with a great info product. There were a ton of online searches for the term *Canadian prescription drugs* but, as far as I could tell, no info products to satisfy those searches! I had no personal knowledge of this area, so I spent a good amount of time doing careful research into all the issues and factors that went into Canadian drugs versus U.S. ones, including when it was possible to substitute generic drugs for brand-name ones and how to find the best Canadian pharmacy.

As I finished the report I licked my chops at the dough I'd soon make. When the time came to put the report online and start to make that money, I discovered one tiny little problem—there were no info products about that topic because the search engine had banned all such info products! Apparently, so much garbage had been published about the topic that the lack of products was not a great opportunity, but instead a great big red flag.

I learned the hard way to do more careful research about what appears to be a super opportunity before pouring substantial time into it.

GET MY CHART

In the pages you've just read you have enough product ideas to last you several lifetimes. I could make this section twice as long with more variations but I'd run the risk of over-whelming you to the point of your eyes glazing over. I'd much rather that you pick one of the concepts above and run with it immediately. Still, I want to give you unbelievable value for your purchase of this book. If you'd like a special Product Idea Generator I've created, then just go to www .sixfiguresecondincome.com and type into the search box the words "idea generator."

CHAPTER 3

How to Create Content Cheaply and Easily

It's not uncommon for people to get all excited about the product possibilities I just covered, only then to become pale at the thought of sitting down and writing. If you're one of them, by the time you're done reading this section you'll no longer be worried about that.

First, let's dispel the notion that all of these info products involve sitting down in front of a keyboard and writing. Multiple ways exist for capturing content, but before we get too deeply into that topic it's important to explain that your info product will go through three stages.

Stage 1: Capture the Raw Content
Stage 2: Edit the Content
Stage 3: Deliver the Content

By breaking the process down into these steps the whole thing becomes less daunting and much more clear.

STAGE 1: CAPTURE THE RAW CONTENT

You have many options for capturing content that will become your info product. Let's look at each one.

Method One: Sit Down and Write

This is a common way and may work well for you, especially if you're writing about something with which you're highly familiar. You can just let 'er rip in front of a keyboard. If you take this option, I highly recommend six principles:

1. Do Not Edit While You Write!

This is probably the biggest cause of writer's block there is. People expect that the words they put on paper from the start need to be clear, grammatically correct, and finished. If you suffer under that expectation you're needlessly suffering.

You are much better off thinking of the writing process more like the clay-sculpture process—you throw a big hunk of clay on a table and start to work it from rough shape to successively finer details. All the raw material goes onto that table from the outset and then it's a matter of cutting away, moving around, stepping back, and smoothing.

Do not allow the censor part of your brain to interfere with the expressive part. Let your expressive part get all that clay onto the table in any which way. Then you can bring the censor out from his locked room to do his thing. You'll need to herd him back into the room when it's time to get more raw material down on paper.

2. Do Not Let Other People Hear or See Your Work While It's in Rough Form

You are probably highly aware of nonverbal and verbal behavior, and the slightest criticism or joke about your work-in-progress could easily mean that you abandon it. I suggest that you get it completely down on paper and edited at least once before showing it to bystanders.

3. I'll Make This Point Again—Do Not Sweat How Long or Short the Document Becomes

If it's much longer than you expected, then you can make decisions during the editing process to cut portions or even turn it into two info products. If it's much shorter then ask yourself if it completely covers the topic. If so, then leave it alone.

I don't know about you, but I get annoyed when I read something that contains obvious filler content. That's the totally boring and common-sense stuff like, "Be sure not to store your gasoline can with an open top next to your furnace." *Oh really! Gee thanks for telling me that—I would never have known.* You're better off keeping your document as short as necessary to cover the content. Your readers might even appreciate the compact, pithy prose.

4. Do Not Become a Slave to Accuracy During the Writing Process

If you don't know a model number, statistic, or other fact, then don't get sidetracked by stopping your writing to look it up. If you're on any kind of a writing roll at all, just keep writing and stick in a spot like this: "And when the time comes to replace the gasket, just order Part Number __ from www._____.com." That way you can fill in the blanks later and not disrupt the thought you were getting down.

5. Just Start, No Matter What

If you sit down and simply cannot get started with any good ideas you'll laugh at this well-known principle among writers—you just start to write, "I don't know what to write. I don't know what to write. I don't know what to write. . . ." By about the tenth time you write that, your brain will unclog and you'll begin to have thoughts somewhat more useful like: "Well, I know the calibration process for the water filter involves something like 11 steps and they are the unpacking, then the. . . ."

If you are patient, pretty soon the words become more descriptive and helpful. Again, do not censor yourself, because you must get the raw material on paper at first, no matter what it takes.

Some people have good success with first writing down what something will not be. For instance: "This guide is not going to be the typical 'how to' book about quilting because by my count there are more than 130 quilting books. Instead, I'm going to assume that you've quilted all your life and want to discover little-known and really uncommon materials you can use. . . ."

6. Make an Outline

Once you realize the power of writing using an outline, you'll never go back. We were all taught boring outlining in English class in school. The schoolmarm might have said, "Children, be sure to outline in just the way I have shown you." No doubt that method involved arbitrary rules about how an outline should be constructed. It's no wonder that you may not have done an outline since fourth grade.

Forget those rules. Think of an outline as simply a way to organize ideas, sentences, or even fragments. First, it allows you to slop down information in whatever order it appears in your brain. Then, it's a quick process to group ideas under main headings or subheadings. After a short period of outlining, your thoughts begin to take on a structure that you may not have anticipated. Depending on the information you've captured, there will be logical groupings. As one area grows too large it will become clear how to break it into smaller units.

By using an outline, your actual information will drive the structure rather than an arbitrary initial plan driving it.

Then, as you write it becomes a simple matter of following your outline and writing about each small fragment. Because the whole document is in logical outline format before you write, you can be fairly confident that the finished product will hang together.

Do not interpret what I just said to mean that you must have a finished outline before you write. The process of writing a book or a smaller info product is *iterative*—you research, then outline, then write, then adjust your outline, then research some more, and so on. Use it like a flexible tool and not some rigid framework.

Microsoft Word has a pretty handy outlining tool that ships right inside the normal software—nothing new to buy. You can access it by going to the *View* tab and then look for *Outline*. I'll tell you right now that it takes perhaps 20 minutes to fumble around with the controls and interface before you get the hang of it.

That means, if you give up before 20 minutes are over, you've given up too soon. The payoff is definitely worth the effort.

Another very good tool is the *MindManager* software program from www.mindjet.com. It's not free or even cheap software but is quite useful. It will create not only outlines but *mind maps*. Those are graphical maps of information, which can also contain pictures, web pages, and other content.

I use the MindManager tool to organize my thoughts about a project, but then I usually move to Microsoft Word to create the detailed outline from which I write. (This book is the result of just that process, by the way.)

Now that we've covered the standard way of getting content—writing it down—let's look at other excellent methods.

Method Two: Have a Conversation

I unscientifically estimate that a minority of people find it easy to sit down and write, but that most people have no trouble carrying on a conversation. If you're in that latter group and not the former, do not consider it a handicap at all.

It's my recommendation to go out and buy a digital audio recorder. My favorite is the *Olympus DS-40 Digital Voice Recorder*. It's about a hundred bucks, though you can get other models and brands for significantly less or more money. You don't need lots of features but you do need good sound quality.

I like this Olympus model because it's small, holds many hours of recordings, has very good sound quality, and the controls are intuitive. It also runs on readily available AAA batteries.

Another option is to record on the phone. I really like my *Plantronics Encore H91N Monaural Headset with Noise Canceling Microphone*, which attaches to a *Plantronics MX-10 Amplifier*. Headsets are wonderful for when you're at the computer and talking with someone. This particular setup allows me to raise or lower the volume and also to mute someone. I can plug the Olympus recorder right into the amplifier and capture everything said on the call. I've recorded hundreds of hours of phone conversations that way and turned them into info products.

You can just put the recorder on the table and talk away. If you're comfortable simply talking out loud to yourself, that's great. It's often more comfortable to have a true conversation with someone on the phone. If that person knows something about the area you're going to focus on, that's all the more content you'll be capturing, but let's assume that only you know about the topic. I suggest you create a short list of topics you want to talk about and just dive in.

As with the writing process, do not censor yourself in the conversation. You're merely getting all that content out into the open. If you need to restate something better, then do it. You may end up cutting out whole sections of what you said and that's fine. Just try to get on a roll and let your thoughts roam over the topic.

If you find your first attempt less than satisfactory, don't give up. Remember that you're experimenting with the best way to generate content and it may take weeks or even months of trying different methods to find one that feels just right.

If you're following this spoken-conversation route, also experiment with different conversation partners. Some people have a way of engaging and asking questions that's far more productive than other people who might as well be potted plants.

You have three options for taking that recorded content and making it usable.

First, you can simply listen to it and write down the sections you find the most helpful. I'm not a fan of that method but you may be.

Second, you can use a tool like *Dragon Naturally Speaking* to have the computer transcribe your words. Speech-recognition software seems to be getting better by the month. What formerly was a pretty cumbersome and inaccurate process of using software to create transcripts has now become fairly workable. With the recent generation of software, the more you train it to understand your voice the more accurate it becomes.

Third, you can hire a person or company to create a transcript of your audio. It's the least amount of work for you and you'll end up with a highly accurate printed

version of what you covered. The cost is somewhere between one and two dollars per minute of recording. Prices
vary depending on how many people are speaking on the
audio, whether they're in a quiet or noisy setting, and how
quickly you want the transcript.

I can refer you to a list of one or more companies that
continue to do a good job. Go to www.sixfiguresecond
income.com and type the word "transcript" into the search
box.

Method Three: Interview People

This is just a variation on the last method. Earlier in this
chapter I suggested that you might interview experts or
even just frequent users of some product in order to get
material. Take your audio recorder along and come prepared with a series of questions.

You can use your judgment about how explicit you are
concerning the topic you'll be turning into an info product.
Many experts are accustomed to being interviewed and are
unlikely to grab your idea—after all, they're already established authorities in that field with ongoing projects.

You should follow the same rules here as you would
about not plagiarizing someone in print. In other words, if
Mary Jones gave you excellent information, be sure either
to quote her or at least indicate that she was a contributor
to your product. You might even put her e-mail or web
address in your material as a way of paying her back.

Frankly, the biggest danger with interviewing people is
that you're unlikely to use this method at all for fear of
someone stealing your idea. Could it happen? Of course.
Can you take the simple precautions I mentioned and
minimize that possibility? Yes. But remember how most
people labor under their own versions of Uncle Moe and

never get around to creating a product for all the reasons we've discussed. You're much more likely to profit from collaborating with other people than you are to run up against them as determined competitors.

Method Four: Record a Presentation

Let's say you're part of a model aircraft group and you've created a particularly long-range control system. It's not a secret but it's also not widely known. You might at some point deliver an informal presentation about your improvements. If you do, be sure to record that presentation because it could be tailor-made for an info product. The same goes for salespeople whose business is to deliver presentations about a new or improved product or service.

I'm not suggesting that you covertly record someone else's presentation and then sell the information. I'm only saying that sometimes the information you're after is not on paper and you haven't captured it through a conversation or an interview, but it does exist in presentation form. If that's the case, you may be in luck because often presentations already have an order and logic to them, thus making your job to organize it easier.

Method Five: Capture Screenshots

I've seen many info products that consist of a series of detailed pictures of computer screens—known as *screenshots*—along with annotations.

With all the buttons and windows on a typical computer screen these days it's often cumbersome to describe to someone exactly where to go to accomplish a task. It's much easier for you—and less frustrating for the user— to see a picture of a computer screen with arrows pointing to the exact spot under discussion.

Though many options exist for capturing those screen-shots, the tool I use is called Snagit by www.techsmith.com. It's not very expensive but can capture an amazing variety of screens. For instance, let's say you want to capture an entire web page but it's a long one, requiring you to scroll down for multiple pages. The Snagit tool can be set to grab the entire web page. You can then annotate the page by adding arrows, text, and other graphics.

Consumers love detailed screenshots like this because they are so self-explanatory. You needn't say "Now go to the upper left area of the screen, right under the little blue box where it says 'For More Information', and then. . . ." Your screenshot will indicate exactly where you mean. If your commentary is too large to fit on the actual screen-shot itself then the program easily allows you to put a big red number or letter there. Then you can refer to that number or letter in your accompanying text below the screenshot.

Method Six: Do a Video Capture of a Web Session

This is like a screenshot on steroids. You can set up your computer to record not only your screen, but an entire session where you move from screen to screen. It will make a movie out of your navigating around the screen and can capture not only the web pages themselves but all your mouse movements and your voice, too.

If you have not seen a web session captured before, you're in for a treat. It can not only save you an enormous amount of time in explaining a process to someone, but it will also spare that person a great deal of frustration. That's another way to say that it's extremely valuable and people will pay you for the information in your video capture.

Remember that Joomla story I told you before, where I paid a guy to find out how to set up the Joomla software? That was just this sort of video capture technology.

Techsmith, the same company that creates the screenshot tool Snagit, also makes a video capture tool called Camtasia. You can also get it at www.techsmith.com. If you go to my site at www.sixfiguresecondincome.com and type "video capture" into the search box, I'll give you my current recommendation for tools that may be comparable to Camtasia but cost less. The technology is rapidly changing.

You're going to need an external microphone to plug into your computer in order to capture your voice as you do the online demonstration. Do not try to use the built-in mic on your computer because it won't sound good enough. I can recommend a good external mic called the *Snowball* by Blue Microphones. They're at www.bluemic.com or you can buy it on Amazon or at many other places on the web. It's not expensive and plugs right into the USB port on your computer. It does an excellent job of capturing voices in crystal-clear fashion.

You may wonder what happens not if but when you mess something up on the video. Yes, it will happen that you forget part of what you're trying to cover or you may garble a few words. You might also say something confusing and wish you had said it differently. No sweat. You'll have all the tools that a Hollywood director would have to fix the problem.

For instance, let's say you said something confusing. Just say that part over again, right during the session. After you finish the recording, you'll be able to edit out the blooper and keep the good part. You can even raise the sound level or chop out the doorbell ringing in the background. The editing capabilities are so feature-rich that you'll only use a fraction of them.

You need to know something else. Your goal is not to make a video that rivals what Steven Spielberg might produce. Of course, it's true that the complexity of television productions has skyrocketed along with technology. You might think that means people would therefore only buy slick productions, but you'd be wrong. In this age when you go to the movies and cannot be sure if the actor you're looking at is real or computer generated, there's actually a greater appreciation for authenticity.

You should make sure that you record your video in a quiet place because it's distracting to have dogs barking and pots and pans banging in the background. But, assuming your sound quality is clear, forget the need for slickness. Instead just go for the image of one person talking to and helping another person.

STAGE 2: EDIT THE CONTENT

Now that you have six different methods for capturing content for your info product, it's time to edit that content into a coherent piece.

By the way, you should aim for substantially more content than you expect to use. At least that's what I do, because it gives me the confidence that I can pick and choose only the best stuff to put in the product.

Make sure that your material flows logically, which again is a reason for creating an outline. Even if you started the project without knowing much about the topic, by this point you will know a lot. You should guard against the expert's predicament of knowing something so well that you skip over details that seem obvious or boring to you.

If you have a clear mental picture of your info product buyers, then keep their skill level constantly in mind. If they're beginners then be very explicit about what to do when.

The very fastest way to lose the attention of beginners is by stumping them early with unclear information. They were getting into your material and everything was going along smoothly when suddenly you used jargon or referred to something they didn't understand. Then, as you continued to refer to it, the beginners again felt lost. Pretty soon they'll just stop going through your stuff and will likely ask for a refund.

You cannot be too detailed with beginners. However, if you've created a detailed piece especially for a relatively knowledgeable audience, you must be careful about boring them. The information that a beginner might find complicated is the same stuff that could be boring to the expert. It could appear to be filler material to them if you're marketing the guide as more advanced, and they could stop reading for that reason.

Therefore, match the complexity and detail to what the audience is asking for. If you did your research before launching the product, you should have a clear idea of that correct level of detail.

Don't be surprised to do a lot of cutting and pasting at this stage. What I do is save all my raw material to an archive document and then make at least one copy of it. I only do editing to the copy. It's a terrible feeling to have created some raw content and then delete that content only to discover later that you want to use it after all but have no backup copy.

Backup Your Work!

I'm somewhat redundant in the number of copies I keep of anything I've created. If you have never had a computer crash—you will. It's inevitable.

Therefore, the first thing you must do to protect yourself in this business is to get a backup solution for your files. Anything is better than nothing. Start by telling your word-processing system to backup your document automatically. That's semi-helpful if the original document becomes corrupted, which is not uncommon.

The only problem is that sooner or later your hard drive will die. Sometimes files can be retrieved from busted hard drives but sometimes not. You're better off having a backup solution that is separate from your hard drive. I have two solutions. First, I have a small external hard drive that at least daily—and automatically—will make copies of anything I've changed on my computer. That external drive is encased in a box that's fire and water proof, for all intents and purposes.

Second, I have a web-based backup program that makes regular copies of all changed files. It's all encrypted and only I have the password, so all that information travels to the web-based company in encrypted form, not openly over the Internet. With that system I'm confident that if anything happened to my whole city I could still access my computer documents from any other web-enabled computer—assuming I remembered the password, of course.

Because these systems are changing and improving so frequently, I hesitate to recommend anything in this book because it could become outdated quickly; therefore, if you want to know the current configuration I recommend, go to www.sixfiguresecondincome.com and type the word "backup" into the search box.

Once you have edited your document, now's the time to think about showing it to someone else to make sure it hangs together for fresh eyes.

Just as you may carefully choose your friends, be careful about choosing your reviewers. You gain nothing from someone who's unconditionally positive regardless of what you put in front of him or her. On the other hand, some people get hung up on style or on nit-picky details. Your reviewer should focus on whether your information is clear or confusing and whether it's complete or not.

You also do not need an expert on the subject matter just yet because that person could get too detailed too quickly. You'll get the expert opinions soon enough so, for now, simply make sure you're on the right track.

STAGE 3: DELIVER THE CONTENT

You have the luxury of choosing from an astonishing array of ways to deliver your content. See Table 3.1.

Wow! Do you see what I mean by "astonishing"? I hope you dog-ear this page and study it because, practically by itself, that chart could make you a fortune.

It's all the rage in our green-focused discussions these days to talk about repurposing things, like the act of turning old tires into shoes and so on. Well, you can do a much more profitable form of repurposing by taking the same content and converting it into products that are differentiated by their delivery media and also comprehensiveness.

Let's look at Table 3.1 in more detail. First, I want to point out that its title is a *Rough Guide* on purpose. There's nothing carved in stone about it. For instance, you may see that a *book* is valued at up to $40. Well, I once bought a book and DVD set from a brilliant fellow and I gladly paid $5,000 for it. His knowledge and experience was so vast that it was worth that amount of money to have his limited-edition, privately published book.

Therefore, do not take anything on the chart to be gospel but simply use it as a starting point for thinking about

TABLE 3.1 Rough Guide to Product Formats and Pricing

	FREE	UP TO $40	$40–$150	$150–$500	OVER $500
Print	1. Special Report 4. Sample Newsletter	Special Report 5. Book 7. Fast-Start Guide 8. Pocket Guide 9. Checklist T-shirt	2. Getting-Started Kit	3. Home Study Course 6. Interview Series Transcript	Home Study Course
Objects	10. T-shirt 11. Poster 13. Calendar	12. Laminated Poster 14. Game 15. Mug 16. Information Wheel			
Audio	17. CD	One or More CDs 18. DVD	Multiple CD Set	Home Study Course 19. Interview series on MP3	

	FREE	UP TO $40	$40–$150	$150–$500	OVER $500
Video	20. Free Video	DVD	One or More DVDs	21. Live Event Videos	Live Event Videos
Phone	22. Toll-free 24/7 Recorded Line	23. Consulting Hotline	24. Teleseminar/ Webinar		
Internet	25. Trial Software 28. Online Calculator 30. Free PDF 31. Free Audio	26. iPhone App	27. Software 29. Interview Series PDFs	Software	
Live	32. Consultation	33. Lunch or Dinner Seminar	34. One-Day Seminar	35. Consultation (Paid Version)	36. Boot Camp Consultation 37. Live Tour 38. Cruise Member Site
Continuity			39. Newsletter 41. Weekly Faxes Software	40. Membership Site	42. Coaching

what you might offer. Also, please do not get overwhelmed by the product forms and mentally shut down, thinking, *"There's no way I can do all this stuff."* You don't need to do even half of it, ever. You could conceivably stick to only a handful of product forms and make a six-figure income. Think of it like a menu where you pick and choose what suits you best.

I've numbered the unique items on this chart but did not number every item because some of the same type of product appears in multiple places. Here are observations about these product forms.

1. Special Report

This is my all-time favorite. I'm quite confident that more millions of dollars have been generated from this type of report than from any other. You should consider it to be a highly effective hook on a fishing line. You hook potential customers by the high-quality information you give them in your free or low-cost special report, and then you reel them in with higher-priced offerings.

Most of my students who eventually pay me $4,000 to attend a three-day live event were people who first learned about me through a special report.

Why would you ever go to the effort of putting together valuable information only to give it away in the form of a free special report? Because people are so inundated with information these days and most of it is garbage. Consumers have developed an effective *BS Radar System* that instantly snaps on when they hear: "And wait! There's more! When you buy my guide to *35 Advanced Sonar Techniques for Catching Great Lakes Fish*, well, those prize-winning fish'll be leaping into your boat by themselves! So order now!!!!"

You know the nonsense I'm talking about because you're probably a victim of it every day. Since when does any product ever become an "Out-of-control ATM spewing money at your feet"? And if for some reason such an opportunity ever existed in nature, why would you be telling me about it? Why wouldn't you just keep it to yourself and become richer than Bill Gates?

The most effective way to counteract this radar system is to remember and act on this principle: *Give Before You Get.*

The snake-oil salesmen want you to get their stuff right away. They tantalize you with a hundred different promises in the hope that one of them resonates with you.

Instead, use the free-sample technique of giving before you ask for something. Give your potential customers something of real obvious value with no strings attached. When you do that, several excellent things happen.

- You separate yourself from all the *Buy Now!* pushy people.
- You demonstrate your expertise in the topic.
- You provide value for nothing, and that builds confidence in potential customers.
- Those customers are left thinking: *"Wow, if all that quality information is what this person has for free, I wonder how good the paid stuff is—it must be really great."*

We talked some time ago about how competitive some markets are. I can guarantee you that, even in the most competitive of marketplaces, the vast majority of vendors will never offer something of value for free. You will stand out in the very best light.

This phenomenon is not limited to just free special reports, of course. If you deliver a free audio download from a web site you might accomplish the same thing. Don't think *either/or*, but instead think *both/and*. There's no one single Silver Bullet, as we established in Chapter 1. Therefore, think about coming out with a special report and later perhaps doing a free audio or video, and so on.

2. Getting–Started Kit

This usually takes the form of a series of special reports, plus perhaps a CD or a DVD, all spread out for prospects to see. The idea is to show lots of material for a fairly low price. High content plus low price is another way to say *high value*. It can simply be a repackaging of other items you offered separately, including free ones.

3. Home–Study Course

This has been the bread-and-butter of the info products business for some time. It's like the *Getting-Started Kit*, only bigger. This will be the biggest product that many people in your customer list will ever buy because they want a complete system but don't have the time or money to invest in a multi-day live event.

The beauty of a home-study course is it can be composed of content you created for other purposes. For instance, you may have offered a teleseminar or one-day event where a number of speakers presented information. Those are products in their own right, but the transcripts can become the basis for your home-study course manual.

It's common for a home-study course to contain a manual in a three-ring binder, plus audio CDs and a few special reports. It doesn't hurt to show a big spread of stuff people will receive for their several hundred bucks.

4. Sample Newsletter

This is again in the spirit of *give before you get*. Why not give people a sample of your existing newsletter and show them what they're missing each month? Some marketers swear by newsletters that are one single page of great content. Other people like to give 12 to 16 pages of good but less-dense content. There's no one right answer and both ends of the spectrum are worth testing.

5. Book

This could really be the topic of several chapters and we won't do that. You know that I like books or you wouldn't be holding one of mine in your hands right now. However, they are a great deal of work for a list price of around $25, especially considering what other, easier products you can sell for $25 or even more.

Still, there's nothing like a book to get wide exposure. It's a great product format for later, after you've already made a bunch of money. On the other hand, if you're particularly itching to become a published author, you need not wait. If that fire is in you to do a book, it just might be the product that puts you on the map.

Just be sure to guard against devoting too much of your time to a book only to become despondent if you get rejected multiple times by publishers. The truth is that publishers will pay much more attention to you once you have a large following of fans. Don't think of a book as a great way to get customers—instead think of a bunch of customers as a great way to get a book deal.

6. Interview Series Transcript

This is more repurposing at work. Some people make tens of thousands of dollars at a time by interviewing a series of experts on a topic and then selling the interviews for $100 to $200, depending on the topic.

If they're smart, they recognize that different people like their information delivered in different media. If I'm a *road warrior* with a long commute each day, I might love to have downloadable MP3 audios of these interviews to listen to instead of the same old news on a radio station.

If I spend a lot of time at a desk, at home, or in airports I might want a handy transcript I can pop out and read with a cup of coffee or while standing in line. Therefore, you can increase the perceived value of an interview by offering both the audio and the transcript.

7. Fast–Start Guide

People are impatient, as you know, and are often willing to pay for the shortest shortcut possible. Marketers sometimes get caught up in a paradox: If they offer a big fat home-study course they're giving lots of value to customers, but they may be overwhelmed when they receive the course in the mail: *"Wow, I don't know where to start with this thing! I bet the first chapter's kind of boring, so I maybe won't start there. Where's the real meat? Did I get myself in over my head again this time? Should I return it instead?"*

You don't want your customers to have those bad thoughts. Therefore, make it easy to take the first few bites of your larger course or system by creating a fast-start guide. It can be nothing more than a summary of what they'll find in other places in your system.

Note: This is typically not something you sell on its own but instead you include it in a larger package and assign a separate dollar value to it, like $49.

8. Pocket Guide

This is a way to take advantage of the downtime people have while waiting in line, eating lunch, and so on. They'll often appreciate that you create your information in many different formats, so whether they're at home, in a car or plane, or just out and about, your material is accessible.

No one person will probably use all the media you provide, but by offering different formats you'll appeal to the broadest possible audience.

9. Checklist

This is an underused category of info product with a lot of potential for you. In a sense, a checklist is the most-distilled type of guide you can have because it answers the request: *Just tell me exactly what I should do when.*

Think about what pilots do before a flight. They've had years of training and we hope they know that airplane inside out. Yet they rely on a preflight checklist to make sure they remembered the procedures in the correct sequence. That method of displaying knowledge can work in other contexts besides aviation.

The other great thing about checklists is they are the opposite of the daunting, giant package of material for someone to have to wade through. They seem simple and inviting and that leaves the correct impression in the minds of your customers.

Often a checklist only makes sense in conjunction with a longer, more descriptive document. You may go into great detail in the longer document about all the variations and possibilities of something and then summarize in the checklist the key actions the reader should take.

10. T-shirt

There's something about T-shirts that animates people. In the course of my (Dave's) dozens of live events around the country, I've offered all sorts of prizes and fun bonuses. T-shirts are definitely one of the most popular.

If you offer a T-shirt, make sure it's a cool one. In other words, if it's a cheapo shirt with plain lettering of your web site name, that's not going to be worn proudly by anyone except you and your mom. You're going to have to spring for a nice design or a well-known quote that resonates with your audience. It's pretty hard to describe a formula in matters of taste, so I won't attempt it. When you hit it right, you'll know because people will buy whatever you have in order to get the bonus T-shirt.

You're not much of a designer? No problem. Just go to www.99designs.com and create a contest. It's a very neat web site that's something of a clearinghouse for people who need designs and designers who need money. You can create a contest for around $100. If you offered $500 it would be considered a lot of money. Then you establish the guidelines of what you're after and set a deadline.

Designers from around the world will create T-shirt designs and post them to your private contest area. You then should critique the contestants' work by saying things like, "You're on the right track here with the alligator motif, but I don't like that color," or whatever your impression is of that work. Your ongoing observations help the designers to get a better sense of what will be a winning entry. By the way, all the designers typically see everyone else's entries so it can become pretty competitive, which is good for you.

At the end of the contest you pick the winner. You get the design sent to you in large, usable format and the designer walks away with the money.

You may feel uneasy about all the other designers who didn't win but that shouldn't bother you. First, no one forced them to compete and they knew the rules. Second, we all know that, in life, *you win some and you lose some*. Third, there's nothing stopping you from hiring one of the other designers for future work if you liked his or her work.

This whole system is just another example of the Internet creating opportunities and value for people. In the bad old days you'd have to pay big bucks for a professional designer at a big firm to create that T-shirt. Fewer designers were employed because even the big firms couldn't hire them all. Now that the middleman is out of the picture, it's a win-win for both the designer and the customer who needs a great design.

11. and 12. Poster and Laminated Poster

People love posters. Similar to checklists, they seem compact, less daunting, and they get right to the heart of a topic. I've had great success with offering posters as either free items to get people to give me their names or as paid products.

I separated these items in the checklist simply because you might offer a free poster that's a downloadable document for people to print out on their own. Then, for perhaps $19 to $49, you can offer to send them a mailing tube with a beautiful, four-color large poster with tons of information on it, professionally designed.

By the way, you could do another contest at www.99 designs.com for the poster. On the other hand, you can go to other sites like www.elance.com, browse the portfolios of graphic designers, and hire one directly without going through the contest route.

Posters can be great products because their brevity works in your favor. Let's say you list on a poster three dozen ways to get something done. That's valuable to the expert who only needed reminding of those methods. However, the beginner might be left wanting more information about those ways. Having your name at the bottom or top of the poster means that anyone viewing it may then contact you and say, "Hey, I saw your poster—do you have more information on those last five items on there?" What a great way to offer motivated people more of your stuff!

13. Calendar

This is not a new concept by any means, but it's just as valuable as it was in the precomputer era. Back then insurance companies and gas stations offered calendars to customers, not because they were just good guys but so that their names literally hung around the house all year.

What could you create that has a nice calendar in it, but also would perhaps subtly remind people of your products and services? If you Google the term *custom calendars* you'll find a huge selection of companies that can do this work in any quantity including very small amounts.

14. Game

Robert Kiyosaki is famous in the real estate and personal wealth arena for coming out with his *Rich Dad Poor Dad* book and his *Cashflow 101* game. What a smart move to think of creating a game in an industry that previously had none.

There's an old story of two shoe salesmen who went to Africa. After the main office back in the United States had not heard from them for months, finally two telegrams arrived. The first one said, "No luck. Coming home. Nobody around here wears shoes." The second salesman's telegram said, "Send boatload of shoes. Nobody around here wears shoes."

It's all how you look at it. Well, Kiyosaki viewed the lack of a game in the personal wealth arena as an opportunity and he became the pioneer. Maybe a game in your chosen product area would work and maybe it wouldn't, but it's worth considering.

15. Mug

This is the same concept as a T-shirt—if it's really attractive, you'll get people to want it as much as the main product you're offering.

16. Information Wheel

Also called *slide charts* and *wheel charts*, these were ancestors to the hand-held computer but they're great even today. Some of them are disk-shaped where you spin one wheel that has little windows punched in it to reveal information on the disk underneath. When you properly line up the windows it provides the answer. Other versions are like paper slide rules, where again you line up several moving cards to arrive at an answer.

If you still don't know what I'm talking about, you can see them in action at: www.alcott.com. They never need batteries and can't be hacked into or infected with online viruses. They're compelling because they are so *retro*. In our hyper-tech age it's almost like going back to an abacus—it makes people stop and think, "*Wow, I haven't seen one of those in decades. Cool!*"

People will not throw them out and are likely to show their friends. It can be an excellent bonus for you to offer alongside your product or it can be a product in its own right.

17. CD

We discussed audio CDs before. You may know that you can also put video on a CD, depending on its length and format. CDs are one of the mainstays of the info product world.

Some manufacturers make tiny round CDs and even ones in the shape of a business card. I suggest you do not bother with these formats because they have been known to damage CD players, and that is the last kind of impression you want to leave with a potential customer.

Of course, technology has advanced beyond CDs to iPods, USB drives, and many other formats. You can also ask a potential customer to download an audio file off the web, saving you the trouble of creating and shipping a CD.

Be very cautious about going down that route because what is easiest to produce often is not the most effective for sales. First, let's consider the road warrior who's an ideal prospect to listen to your stuff during his long commute. Virtually all cars now have CD players, but if you ship your product or special report on a USB drive, only a fraction of cars have ports for them.

Similarly, if you get your prospect all excited to listen to your audio but then ask him to download it, will he bother to? And if he does, the next morning he'll be running late for work. Do you really think he'll remember to hook up whatever needs hooking up in order for your download to play in his car? You better not assume all your prospects are tech-savvy or you'll be greatly disappointed in the response.

For the time being you're safe to ship CDs. Consider it the minimum requirement but you're free to have alternatives where you give customers or prospects the choice of CD, USB drive, or download. It's more work for you but more convenient for customers. Besides, any competitors you have will not bother to do the work, thus giving you yet another competitive advantage.

18. DVD

DVDs share many of the same characteristics as CDs but here are the distinctions: DVDs are only slightly more expensive than CDs and they hold a lot more information. The bigger issue with DVDs is that only a fraction of cars on the road have DVD players. Even if all the vehicles on the road had DVDs they're not as user-friendly as CDs because you can hardly expect drivers to peer closely at the tiny screen to see what your mouse is doing on the web page you're showing. Even if you have Hollywood-quality video on your DVD, again you have the distracted-driver matter to contend with.

It doesn't get too much better at home, unfortunately. After the novelty of DVDs wore off, marketers realized that many customers just can't be bothered with sitting in front of a computer or DVD player for hours, watching video. They're so accustomed to great-quality video via television that all but the most devoted followers get bored and turn off the DVD somewhere in the first disk.

Here's the bottom line for you: Don't rely solely on DVDs to deliver your content, but make sure that you give people options to hear just the audio portion of the DVD via CD, or perhaps get a transcript of the session along with printed screenshots of any important visuals.

19. Interview Series on MP3

I touched on a version of this earlier in Number 6. You can add value to a series of interviews by making them available not only in transcript form but in both MP3 downloadable form and even as CDs to be shipped to the customer as well.

20. Free Video

Online videos have become wildly popular in recent years, what with YouTube and hundreds of other places to view free videos. Therefore, the fact that they are free is about as impressive as saying, "Congratulations! You've won the right to make a free local phone call." Big deal. We'll talk more about free video in the lead-generation section, but here I'll just say this: If you make sure that your video gives some really solid or really entertaining content, it can be a major boost to your online efforts.

21. Live Event Videos

This can be a great product to give to people who don't have the time or money to attend one of your multi-day live events. However, here's a major warning: If you take an entire live event and reduce it to videos, you run a major risk of cannibalizing the sales of your live event.

Here's what happens: Joe is thinking of going to your three-day event in Chicago but isn't sure he can swing the cost. If your event is compelling enough, he just might get creative and cobble together the money and vacation time so he can go.

Now you come out with a DVD set of your last event, and three bad things happen.

Bad Thing Number One

Joe decides: Hey great! I don't need to go to that $4,000 event after all! I can just sit at home and watch the DVD set for $500. I'll buy it. In some cases, Joe couldn't ever have gone to your event so you made $500 on him rather than zero. You can also be sure that in other cases you would have had Joe at $4,000 and now you'll get only $500.

Bad Thing Number Two
The DVDs sit in Joe's office and he never watches them. Oh, he wanted to and hoped to, but there always was something more pressing than to glue his butt in that seat and study the DVDs. The less Joe gets into the DVDs and learns the system, of course the less benefit they are to him, which means he's more likely to refund the product purchase.

That's one of the great benefits of getting people to be at a live event—you have their full attention, more or less. They get caught up in the enthusiasm of others and hear all the other peoples' questions and then the answers. They get immersed in the subject matter in a way that is extremely rare for the home-study course person to accomplish. You will indeed find some people who really do grab the bull by the horns and extract value from every page of a home-study kit, but it's less common.

Bad Thing Number Three
Mary just went to your live event last month and thought it was pretty good. She met a number of valuable contacts and got all her questions answered. Then she went online and discovered that the videos of her event are selling for $500 and not the $4,000 she paid to attend live.

What should Mary conclude? She should think to herself, "That's okay. If I got the home study videos I probably would have never watched them and certainly would not have had all my questions answered. Besides, I wouldn't have met those people from Missouri who will be great to do business with."

That's what she should think, but this is what she does think: "How dare they sell the event videos for 500 bucks! I paid 4 grand for that event and now most of it is right there on DVDs. I got ripped off!"

Whereupon, Mary goes onto every blog she can find and announces how you've ripped off her and the other seminar attendees with your new DVD set.

I would be extremely careful about offering the full set of videos from an event. It's okay to sell highlights of the event so people get a mixture of content and also the awareness that they missed out on a lot of stuff.

The only other situation where you might contemplate actually offering the entire thing on video is if you're certain that you'll never hold it again. Even then I'd wait a while after the last live event so you don't have angry customers who recently paid much more for the live version.

22. Toll–Free 24/7 Recorded Line

I'm a big fan of this method of presenting information. Years ago it was about as automated as things got, but it's another under-used method today.

Some people learn best by reading. They're called *visual learners*. Others learn best by hearing, in which case they're called *auditory learners*. Still others like to have information sink in by doing, and they're called *kinesthetic learners*.

If you only send people to a web site, most likely they'll be most influenced if they're visual learners. Yes, you can have audio on your site, and I would recommend that, but also keep in mind that many people are still more comfortable with the telephone than they are with a computer.

That's where the 24/7 prerecorded line comes in. On your web site, business card, and any other kind of advertisement you should give out the phone number for that line. Be certain that you state clearly that the line is *prerecorded*. Otherwise, people may think they'll be grabbed by a slick telephone sales shark when they call the number and will be made to buy something they don't want. The prerecorded nature of the line is very nonthreatening for people who want to know more but don't want to engage with anyone just yet.

When people call the number, be sure to give them good solid information, just as I've recommended for special reports. Here's where it gets really interesting. After your initial message, now divide your audience by saying, "Press one if you'd like to hear more tips about how to install window burglar sensors, press two if you want to hear more about how to install garage door burglar sensors. . . ."

The great thing is that by the numbers they press you will gather further information on the topic that most interests them. That's valuable because you can then give them more of that specific topic later. If you notice that lots of people press number five, well, what products do you have to satisfy that targeted need?

At the end of each message, no matter which button they pressed, you should have an option for them to press "0" to get to someone live. You will find that a certain number of people are ready right now to take action and buy your stuff. Do not let them cool off by shunting them to a recording!

Even if you cannot personally take the live message any time of the day or night, you still have choices: You can hire answering services to do the order-taking for you, or perhaps you know people who work from home and would be delighted to make some additional money by answering occasional calls and taking orders.

If you want to find out my current recommendation for companies that offer this kind of service quite inexpensively, just go to www.sixfiguresecondincome.com and type "recorded line" into the search box.

23. Consulting Hotline

Could it work for both the vendor and the customer to provide a little bit of help for a little bit of money? Yes, it can and one way is through this type of phone number. I've seen the system work where someone buys a consultant's time in 15 minute increments—even just one 15-minute block. Then they schedule a call and deliver the advice.

An entire industry is growing around this concept. Check out www.liveperson.com. It has over 30,000 experts in its database and each one sets a price for the consultation. It might be a per-minute rate or some kind of flat rate. You can either have an online chat session with the expert or communicate via e-mail or by phone.

Naturally, this might not be the very first revenue model you choose to try out because you may or may not be expert at anything right now. If you are, then this service might be something that could make you money and get you immediate exposure without even needing to put together a web site or look for clients because *LivePerson* does all that.

If you aren't yet expert at something you should consider using this service as a way of paying to interview experts for an info product you're building. It's a clever service.

24. Teleseminar/Webinar

I cannot stress strongly enough what superb tools teleseminars and webinars are for building an info product business.

With a teleseminar you get a group of people on the phone for between 45 minutes and 2 hours to listen to you either interview someone, be interviewed by someone, or make a presentation. A webinar is the same thing except you give people the option of following along on their computers. They listen to you on the phone but their computers are logged into a special service that allows them to see your computer desktop.

Let's talk about why teleseminars are such fantastic tools and then we'll discuss webinars.

A. Teleseminars Are the Most Inexpensive Way for You to Deliver Live Content

Words on paper are great for many things, including the book you're reading right now. But if I were discussing the topic of teleseminars right now with you on the phone, you might be even more engaged in the topic. People are naturally attracted to conversations.

B. Teleseminars Can Be Intimate in the Proper Sense

If you're good at delivering content via teleseminar, then each member of the audience feels like you're talking only to him or her. This is powerful! When I have hundreds of people in my boot camp audience it's of course impossible for me to be up on stage and deliver the feeling that I'm talking to one single person. I can walk around, make eye contact, and shake your hand and all of that is helpful—but you still know you're in a big audience.

With the teleseminar I can make you feel like just you and I are on the line. I may not be referring to you by name but I can still talk to you directly. If my material is interesting to you, I'll keep your attention for the whole time.

C. The Teleseminar Can Be as Active or Passive as You Want It to Be

You can choose to have a lively question-and-answer discussion on a call where everyone participates, or it can be an audience listening to two people in an interview, or it can simply be one person delivering a message to the audience. The best method depends on the group that's on the call. My favorite type of call is the interview because there's a lot of energy when you get a good interviewer together with a good expert.

D. You Can Record the Call Once and Play It Back Multiple Times

As long as you take simple precautions, your call can become *evergreen* as they say in the business. When you record the call, do not include small-talk like, "Wow, that Super Bowl game was something, huh." That dates you as having delivered the call in the winter. If you do intend to use a call again, just edit out those sections and the call can become effectively timeless. That means you can do the work once and get the benefit again and again. It doesn't get better than that.

E. Your Audience Doesn't Need to Know How Many Other People Are on the Line

Let's say you are starting a new type of info product and you have not yet built up a large list of prospects. You could conduct a teleseminar where only one person was on the line—or even no one else was on the line—but as far as listeners were concerned, it might have been hundreds. I'm not suggesting that you lie to listeners, but you simply need not tell them how many other people are on the line.

This is excellent for the person just starting in a business. Compare that to running the risk of renting a room at the local hotel and trying to fill it for a live presentation. You might be very successful at packing them in, but what if there's a blizzard or some major news event that day? You paid for the room, and your dad and one other person showed up.

If you had conducted the teleseminar and recorded it, then your dad and that one person would still have received good value for the call but you could later replay the call for lots of people.

* * *

As great as teleseminars are, webinars can add even one more dimension to your presentation—those visual learners now can see your presentation as well as hear you. When I'm in the early stages of an info product I may not yet have a polished visual presentation, in which case I'll do a teleseminar. But after I assemble interesting visuals like pictures, screenshots, and PowerPoint presentations I usually move to the webinar format.

Note: As I described earlier with DVDs, it's dangerous to assume that your customers or prospects are all sitting in front of their computers, nondistracted and ready to absorb your material. Therefore, it's important to design a webinar to be effective for people who might call in and listen to your presentation while driving. You'll quickly lose them if all they hear is, "Okay now go to the top right portion of your screen. . . ."

 Warning: Do NOT Open Up the Lines So Everyone Can Hear Everyone Else!

I can tell you from doing literally hundreds of teleseminars that this is a prescription for great suffering on the part of listeners—and for poor results too. The more people you have on the line, the more you'll hear an absolute cacophony of dogs barking, car horns honking, dishes clanking, babies crying, and the very worst—someone who calls into your line and puts you on hold so the entire call gets treated to elevator music.

You simply must put yourself in *conference mode* where all the callers can hear you but only you can speak. Later in the call if you choose to open up the lines for questions, the technology exists for you to let people speak in an orderly fashion.

Remember the concept of *repurposing*: Once you deliver the teleseminar or webinar you can get a transcript made of the presentation and sell that along with the audio of the call.

If you want to know the systems I use these days for conducting teleseminars and webinars, just go to www .sixfiguresecondincome.com and type "teleseminar" into the search box.

25. Trial Software

The expectation bar has been raised in the world of software. Few people are willing these days to take a gamble on installing semi-functional software during a trial period. They want instead to see the software work in its full-featured form before deciding whether to buy it. If you ever are in a position to offer software for sale, that's the way to go.

26. iPhone Application

I refer to the iPhone only because it's the leader in having separate applications written for the phone, but of course the *BlackBerry* and other phones also are active in this area. Just a short time ago there were few good phone software applications—or *apps* for short—but things have rapidly changed as the phones have become more capable.

Now it's possible to hire a geek and have an app written for phones for about the cost of having a T-shirt designed. Because apps are a relatively new phenomenon, they have a certain *cachet* or coolness about them. Instead of quickly concluding "*My situation's different,*" you'd be smart to ponder if your info product might benefit from an app. Maybe it's a quick calculator or a database to look up information that varies by region, city, or time of year.

Offering your app for free could bring you many new prospects for your product. If the app is good enough, you could charge somewhere between 99 cents and $19.99 for it.

27. Software

This is no different from trial software in Number 25, but you could consider offering software that requires payment up front but that carries a full guarantee if the customer decides to return it.

It's worth noting that current software is moving away from the model that prevailed in the last several decades, where you buy a box of software and install it on your computer. The trend now is to pay for access to software that's available on the web with nothing to install on your end. This removes a major headache for customers who become extremely frustrated and angry about installation problems. It also allows you to make quick upgrades to the software without shipping piles of disks and incurring more installation-support headaches.

28. Online Calculator

You know those postal mail promotions where on the order form it asks you to take a sticker from one spot and place it on another spot? Those companies are not being silly or arbitrary but are incorporating what's known as an *involvement device*.

Whenever you can involve a prospect in a physical act it helps to increase attention and sales. Online calculators are great involvement devices even if you offer them for free. Popular ones have included "What's your REAL age?" This tool asks you a series of questions to determine how old you act versus how old you really are. Other involvement devices calculate something related to weight loss or your likelihood of finding your true love.

It's good practice to have prospects use the calculator without your asking for any name or other contact information. Then in order for prospects to see the answer, you ask for a name and valid e-mail address and send the answer to that e-mail address. This system ensures that you do not have people typing in test@test.com as their e-mail address simply for the sake of getting to the next screen with the answer.

As with iPhone apps, it's definitely worth thinking about what type of calculator you could offer.

29. Interview Series PDFs

I've already spoken about this excellent product, but just in case you're not sure what a "PDF" is, that term stands for *Portable Document Format*. It's now a practically universal method for displaying a document online because it works on just about any kind of computer brand under the sun and the reader tool is a free download. It's superior to sending a Microsoft Word document to customers because they may not own that software.

30. Free PDF

Nothing much to say here other than it's a good way of delivering content before you ask for money.

31. Free Audio

Similar to a free PDF, a free audio interview or presentation is an excellent way to hook people in the good sense of the word. They can hear your voice and decide if they like the content you deliver. It could be as short as 10 minutes or a full-blown hour-long interview.

32. Consultation

This is more of an advanced tool for when you have trained consultants on your staff. I (Dave) offer free consultations in my real estate investing business because many prospects aren't sure if they're cut out to be investors. By offering them a free 30-minute consultation, they get to ask their questions of one of my staff and they'll get customized answers.

Does it cost me good money to hire and train those staff members? Yes. Do some of the prospects end up concluding that real estate investing is indeed not for them? Yes. But it's a good way to *give before you get*, as we discussed before. Besides, it often helps people who are stuck at the stage of *my situation's different*—during the consultation they get a chance to explain their situation and we determine if it is in fact compatible with real estate investing.

33. Lunch or Dinner Seminar

This is another advanced technique for when you have an established product or service. What you do is send invitations either to prospects on your list, or to new names you get through advertising, or both. They get to attend a free lunch or dinner where you describe the product or service and take questions. If the event is constructed property it can work really well to give people a chance to get to know you before they buy.

34. One–Day Seminar

This is the same as Number 33 above, but it is often held on a Saturday. It's usually a good practice to charge people around $99 to attend and then you can either keep that money for all the value you'll deliver, or you can refund it when they show up. If you've gone to the effort to reserve a room and set up a day-long event, you don't want people to sign up for free and then have no hesitation to cancel on you at the last minute or simply become a *no-show*. The $99 returnable deposit helps to prevent that situation.

35. Consultation (Paid Version)

After you launch a product or service you should consider establishing an hourly rate for consultations. Some people not only are convinced that their situation is different from everyone else's but they have no time or inclination to go through a home-study course or live event. They simply want to hire you.

They can turn into great clients if you're willing to do this one-on-one work. I suggest that at some price you might want to be willing. One fellow I know charges $10,000 per hour for consultations. You may not start out at that number but it does have a nice round quality to it; wouldn't you agree?

I recommend that you get paid up front. If you're starting in the business and have not built a reputation, then one way to land more of these consultations is to say, "I know we haven't worked together before and you may wonder if you'll get your money's worth during our call. It's my practice to offer a full refund at the end of this first call if for some reason it was different from what you expected." You'll find that almost no one will ask for a refund.

By the way, the refund concept only applies to the first call because we can assume if they hire you for a second call then they are happy customers.

36. Boot Camp

They're also called *live events*, *success events*, *summits*, and many other creative names. I could write an entire book on this topic because I've conducted so many of them, but suffice it to say that boot camps can be extremely effective for both your students and your revenues.

I've already described how students get the chance to hear directly from you for multiple days and get every one of their questions answered. If they're on the shy side, then they can sit back and hear other people's questions and the responses. They have a chance to focus exclusively on your content for days and work through case histories, problems, and maybe even some role-play sessions. They also can network with other like-minded people.

If you offer a boot camp be sure to video record all your presentations. Then you'll have the luxury of deciding which pieces to use as video highlights, audio snippets, or transcripts.

I already warned you in Number 21 about selling the whole boot camp on DVD or any other format, but it's a good practice to sell portions of the event or just give some of it away as proof of the quality content they'll get when they come to the next one.

37. Live Tour

I don't know your target industry but certain ones lend themselves to creating a buying tour. Certainly in real estate investing it's common to have people come to a special boot camp that is not simply held at a hotel. Instead, your students get on a bus and are driven around a city to look at properties with the intention that they may invest in one or more of them. It's an interesting hands-on approach where they can see you and other experts in action rather than sit in a classroom, though you may also hold part of the event in a seminar setting.

This same concept is used in the photography business where aspiring photographers go to a scenic location and watch as professionals tell them how to take the best photographs. This format could be used for antique tours, woodworking events, fishing competitions, and so on.

38. Cruise

Some marketers regularly organize mid-winter cruises to warm destinations. They conduct classes onboard the ship while it travels from one port to the next, and people can relax and mingle in a fun setting.

As with boot camps and live tours, these events are often conducted not by one presenter but by a team. You might organize the event but have other people in your industry help you to teach it. They take some of the presenting burden off your shoulders and they also may have good products and services to offer the group. You'll get a portion of the profits from their sales and that can add up to substantial dollars for you.

THE EXCELLENT CONCEPT OF CONTINUITY

Continuity is one of the sweetest words an info marketer can hear. It means you offer a product or service in which you are paid by the same customer, typically on a monthly basis—for a long time. Let's look more closely at continuity and the major forms it takes.

39. Newsletter

This is a superb way to build an info-product business. As I said before, your newsletter might be only 1 page or it could extend to 12 or more pages. The idea is to give customers regular, up-to-date information in easily digestible form. It's not a big binder or daunting set of DVDs but rather an almost chatty overview of what's new since the last edition.

Your newsletter should be a combination of new techniques, new applications for old techniques, questions and answers, common problems and their solutions, and commentary on the current marketplace. The current topic for tomato growers might be the new organic insecticide that was a big phenomenon last year and how it's working for gardeners. You get the idea.

Don't concern yourself with making your newsletter look slick—it's just not necessary. Many publications already are so slick that in an odd way you can stand out by looking plain and typewriter-written. I know marketers who run multi-million-dollar newsletter empires in just this format.

Another wonderful aspect of newsletters is that, because people are paying you for them, they pay more attention to your message. Open-minded readers are good candidates for other products and services that may help them. You can piggyback a sales message along with your good regular content and it's likely to be read more and acted upon more than a standalone sales letter.

It's a good practice to have your newsletter readers take some simple action in every edition. You may want them to respond to a survey, submit their entry to a contest, or buy something that's offered under a special deal for newsletter subscribers only. Having them take action every month is a good way to get them accustomed to taking action when you do want them to attend an event or buy something in the future.

40. Membership Site

If done correctly a single membership site can be your main source for a substantial income. It combines the regularity of a newsletter with the ability for members to log in and discuss topics as a group. Some sites also have free services for members only like online tools, free products to members, and other freebies.

I'm not telling you anything new when I say that people enjoy the feeling of belonging to something. Membership sites can foster a sense of community if they have a well-run online forum. By *well-run* I mean not the typical online forum, which is a free-for-all for blabbermouths to shout their opinions on every conceivable topic. Useful forums tend to have moderators whose regular job is to make sure questions get answered and no one gets too personal.

41. Weekly Faxes

This is a variation on the newsletter concept. Either as a standalone product or as part of a larger membership program you can offer a fax to be delivered weekly to the subscriber. Of course, these days e-mail is every bit as fast as a fax, but e-mail is also filled with so much spam that it's a challenge to get through. A fax has the speed of an e-mail but it becomes a physical object that may be more likely to be read and passed around. As with everything else in this book, it's an option you may want to test.

42. Coaching

It's not uncommon for established coaches to make six-figure and sometimes seven-figure yearly incomes. It goes without saying that to make a lot of money you should be providing substantial value, but the beauty of coaching is its efficiency.

At first your coaching might be mainly one-on-one arrangements, but over time that can change. You may have the occasional private coaching session with someone, but most of the calls can be one-to-many affairs with one coach speaking to a group of people.

This can work well because each coaching student gets to hear everyone else's successes, ideas, challenges, and questions. The calls can really take on a community feeling as those dozen or so people get to know each other and work together over time.

Coaching is a great product to offer during one of your live events, like a boot camp. It tends to be more expensive than other products but also is more customized to the needs of the coaching students. When assembling people into a coaching group it's important to have them be at roughly comparable levels of experience. Otherwise, you run the risk of boring the more-experienced members and overwhelming the less-experienced ones.

As you really grow, you can move to the role of supervising other people who become coaches—they're often your most successful students. They know your system cold and also know the challenges students face. They become walking success stories for your system and are worth the profits you'll share with them.

I hope I've succeeded in overwhelming you not with a sense of work but with the amount of opportunity that's at your feet, waiting for you to pick it up.

No doubt you've been aware of many of these product formats and ideas but probably not all of them. This chapter is worth reviewing again and again because it should become your brainstorm-igniter.

THE OPPORTUNITY ENGINEER

Zen Buddhism believes in the concept of a flash of enlight-
enment, where the student meditates for long periods and
eventually—in a flash—achieves a deeper level of consciousness and understanding.

I don't want to turn you into a Zen Buddhist but I do want
to turn you into an *opportunity engineer*. Using the chapter
we've just gone through and the ones ahead, I want you to
have a deeper awareness of the astonishing opportunity for
profit all around you.

While others wallow in self-pity and claim that their
situations are different, you'll be seeing candidates for info
products all around you.

How will you know you've arrived? You'll see other
products and services and will think to yourself, "*Now
that was clever but they could make more money if they
just added this twist. . . .*"

In fact, you'll see so much opportunity that your challenge will be to determine which one deserves your time and
attention. That's a nice problem to have.

Assuming you have at least one great product idea and
you've advanced far enough that you're ready to market it,
the next step is to announce it to the world. You need to get
yourself *open for business* and that's exactly what the
following chapter is about.

CHAPTER 4

Getting Open for Business

Getting a web site online is much easier than you may have been led to believe. Plenty of companies want you to think that it will cost you hundreds of dollars per month to have a web site.

Other companies will assure you that any worthwhile site must be professionally designed from the ground up and they're just the ones to do that for you—for an outrageous fee.

Before reading this book you may have already had ideas about selling your stuff online but were put off by how complicated it sounded to do it right. If that's the case you're going to love this chapter because we'll set you up with a nice web site for a very nice low price. Along the way we'll dispel a number of myths and set the record straight. As with all the advice you'll read in this book, none of it is theory but it's instead what I've used to build web sites and make millions of dollars from them.

THE SEVEN BASIC BUILDING BLOCKS TO A GOOD WEB SITE

 Building Block One: You Need to Own a Good Domain Name

Before you can have a web site you really need a good web address, also known as a *domain name*. Right off the bat we have a myth to bust.

Myth Alert: "All Good Domain Names Are Taken"

I don't care how competitive a market you're in, that's just nonsense. It's either spoken by people who want to keep the competition down or people who have no imagination or creativity.

I agree that all the obvious stuff is taken like *business. com* or *cars.com*. No big deal. The problem with really broad names is they tend to attract a far too general group of customers. If I knew nothing of what's at the site *cars. com* and typed in that term, what might I expect to find there? A Ford dealership? A car-buying web site? A used-car lot? Maybe a car-part online-warehouse? A consumer-safety site with recall notices and crash test results? The list is endless and it's the same problem with other really general domain names.

Profit Principle

People who are on the Internet to browse around and *see what's out there* tend to type in general, one-word and two-word terms. People who are motivated to buy a product or look for a solution tend to type in highly specific terms.

Using our car example, if someone types in *cars.com*, that person either already knows what's on that site or is just browsing around. However, if someone types in *2010 Honda Odyssey EX-L in Ocean Mist Metallic*, do you suppose that person is just aimlessly browsing? I don't think so. You have someone who's already done a lot of research and most likely is shopping for price or availability. That has implications for the sort of descriptive domain name you might want to have.

The book you're currently reading is not about maximizing the amount of traffic you get to your web site. If that's all you want, why didn't you say so? That's easy! Just advertise *Free Beer* and you'll get all the traffic you could ever want. Instead, this book is about getting highly targeted traffic to your site so we can get your product or service sold and make you a pile of money.

Because so many of your very best prospective customers are the ones typing in detailed search terms, that's why not all the good domain names are taken. It just takes a system for smoking out the good names and that's precisely what I'll now lay out for you. First, let's discuss a series of rules that I recommend you follow when picking a domain name.

Rule Number One: Stick with ".com" Names

To explain why I say that, let's think about what happens when you're driving on the freeway and see a billboard. You're doing 60 miles per hour and have a few seconds to notice the cute babe on the billboard and you see the phone number: *1-888-Hot-Club.*

"Okay, I'm gonna call that number as soon as I get home," you think to yourself. Because you know that you don't always remember stuff correctly you even repeat to yourself a couple of times *"Hot Club . . . Hot Club. . . ."*

You get home and after taking off your coat you sit down and are pleased that you remembered the number, so you dial *1-800-Hot-Club.*

It's a *hot club* all right, but not the one you saw on the billboard. No, it's a competitor's hot club. You SAW an *888 number* and REMEMBERED an *800 number* because you're so accustomed to associating 800 numbers with toll-free numbers.

It's no different with domain names. That billboard could just as well have advertised *hotclub.net* and you would most likely have gone home and typed in *hotclub .com.* Do you really want to go to all the effort to advertise with a non ".com" ending only to have a portion of your audience remember someone else's domain name? That's free advertising for them and bad news for you.

Rule Number Two: No Funky Spellings

The same ".com" phenomenon applies to crazy spellings in domain names. If an unimaginative person wants the name "homesforsaleboston.com" and discovers it's been taken, he'll grab "homes4saleboston.com" or even worse "homez 4saleboston.com." He thinks, *So what? I can spell it for people and, besides, I've seen lots of domain names with a '4' instead of a 'for'.*"

He is destined for web failure, and so are almost all the other people with a "4" instead of a "for" or a "u" instead of a "you." Their customers are not going to remember that nonsense and will type the standard version instead.

Some people may tell you that funky, complicated names don't matter because most people don't type names into their computers but they merely click on them.

Certainly, it's true that many domain names get clicked on and not typed in, but why handicap yourself? If your site is popular and one person is telling her friends all about you, why risk having your name garbled at the very time you're trying to spread it far and wide?

Rule Number Three: Try to Anticipate Alternative Spellings and Either Buy Those Names or Avoid Those Words

I was watching the network news recently and this particular show had seven million viewers on an average night. The host garbled a domain name of the guest because the guest mumbled it and the host did not hear that the name included a "the" at the beginning of it so he gave out the incorrect address. That was a superb opportunity for traffic—ruined.

Therefore, if you've found a great restaurant domain name like "thebeststeaks.com" you had better check to see if "beststeaks.com" is available and vice versa. If you only own one of those versions the chances are excellent that the owner of the other name will get some of your traffic. Perhaps you'll get some of his, but that may not be a good tradeoff.

It's the same with terms where the plural and singular forms are common or terms that are frequently misspelled. If you can get the name "TallestSunflowerSeed.com" then also grab "TallestSunflowerSeeds.com." Get both "DelectablePies.com" and "DelectiblePies.com." Then you can easily have the misspelled version redirected automatically behind the scenes to the correctly spelled one.

Rule Number Four: Try to Avoid Hyphens in the Name

This is not as firm a rule as the first two, because Google and other search engines interpret a hyphen as being the same as a space. Therefore, if you're trying to grab *hollywood-homes .com* because someone else has *hollywoodhomes.com*, then you may not have harmed yourself too much. On the other hand, the nonhyphenated name could possibly be what people mainly remember. The other problem with hyphens is you'll forever have to explain to people: "Okay, it's hollywood dash homes.com not hollywoodhomes.com . . . remember there's a dash in there, you know a hyphen? . . . like that little minus sign?" It gets old really fast to explain a name all day long.

Rule Number Five: Think about Customer Benefits, Not about Yourself

Maybe you spent a great many years in school and are proud of the letters after your name, but resist the urge to screw up your domain name due to your pride.

As you'll read later in the section on writing your sales material, most people are tuned to the radio station *WII-fm*. That stands for *What's In It For Me*. They do not care that you have multiple letters after your name—all they know is that their tooth hurts and they would like it to stop hurting. Therefore, if you have a "DDS" degree, an "FAGD," and even an "FICOI" designation, do not clutter your domain name with www.johnsmithddsfagdficoi .com. They will not understand what that stuff is after your name, but chances are excellent they'll type it in wrong.

Dr. Smith would be much better served by naming his site: *SmithSmiles.com* or *SmilesBySmith.com*. That's a benefit his patients will remember and be able to type.

In addition to domain names with benefits like *Organic TomatoSecrets.com* or *FastPerfectPies.com*, another good term to include is a geographic name. So if *OrganicTomato Secrets.com* is taken and your info product is focused on how to grow in the cold New England environment, then look for *NewEnglandTomatoSecrets.com*.

Try This Domain Name Technique

If you're searching for a great name and have had no luck— especially when you follow my rules above—here's something that works well.

It all starts with thinking about domain names as a pattern in three parts—a beginning, a middle, and an end. Each part has a certain function.

Before we look at an example, I want to mention that it's almost always okay to capitalize letters in a domain name because the Internet removes the capitalizations and displays the names in all lowercase letters. The benefit of writing them with capitalized letters to start each word is they're more easily read by people. Occasionally, computers will be picky about capitalizations, so just check if your capitalized domain name works on your site before publishing it on business cards or elsewhere.

Now look at the example of *OrganicTomatoSecrets.com* and let's dissect its parts:

Part One is a prefix of *Organic*. Part Two is the middle section describing the main topic of *Tomato*. Part Three is a suffix of *Secrets*. Let's start a little table with that information:

Prefix	Main Topic	Suffix
Organic	Tomato	Secrets

I left the ".com" part out because we know to use only ".com" endings, so that's a given.

Now let's assume that OrganicTomatoSecrets.com is taken and we need to find a great term for our info product. Here's what you do: Start thinking of other prefixes that could possibly work.

SuperOrganic
Healthy
Healthful
Wholesome
NonChemical
Powerful

Think of alternatives and use a thesaurus if necessary. I like the online tool at www.visualthesaurus.com but a book or other online service is fine too. Now load those terms into the first column and move onto the second column.

Because the second column is for your main topic there will be less room for creativity. Still, depending on your actual info product you might come up with:

TomatoPlant
CherryTomato
BeefsteakTomato

Load those terms into the table and move onto column three. What might be similar to the suffix *Secrets*? How about:

Tips
Techniques
Methods
System
Solutions
KnowHow

When you're done loading into the table all the words for all of the columns your table should look like this:

Prefix	Main Topic	Suffix
Organic	*Tomato*	*Secrets*
SuperOrganic	TomatoPlant	Tips
Healthy	CherryTomato	Techniques
Healthful	BeefsteakTomato	Methods
Wholesome		System
NonChemical		Solutions
Powerful		KnowHow

Now is when things really take off, thanks to a little mathematical concept called the *permutation*. That refers to the process of creating every possible combination from the terms above. In other words, any possible prefix can go with any possible main topic and any suffix. Things still must stay in their proper column sequence—you cannot move a suffix to the front or a prefix to the end—but otherwise you're looking for all combinations.

Don't sweat the tedious work because a few mouse clicks will do all the work for you. Go to www.sixfiguresecond income.com and type the term "permutation" into the search box. I'm not listing the name here because these permutation tools frequently change.

Now you should see a tool that allows you to stick your first-column candidates into its first column and then you can do the same for the other two columns. It should end up looking like Figure 4.1.

Three Important Notes

1. Be sure not to use spaces between words! Domain names cannot have spaces so it must be *Cherry-Tomato* and not *Cherry Tomato*.
2. Also make sure to include the original terms in your list, so put the word *Organic* into your first column and so forth. That's because, even if the original term *OrganicTomatoSecrets* was taken, *OrganicTomato-Methods* may be available.
3. Be sure to put the ".com" part not in the third column but in the special place in the tool where you can ask for it to appear after every single combination. In Figure 4.1 it's called *Divider 3.*

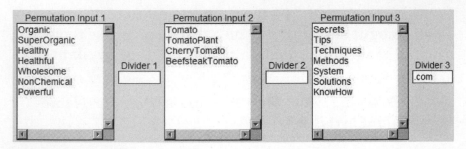

FIGURE 4.1   Make Your Work Easy With a Permutation Tool

Now hit the *Generate Permutations* button or whatever it's called on the tool. If you properly loaded in the terms above, you will instantly see a list of 196 possible domain names! It will have alphabetized your terms and displayed the results as follows:

HealthfulBeefsteakTomatoKnowHow.com
HealthfulBeefsteakTomatoMethods.com
HealthfulBeefsteakTomatoSecrets.com
HealthfulBeefsteakTomatoSolutions.com . . .

At the end of the list you'll see:

WholesomeTomatoSystem.com
WholesomeTomatoTechniques.com
WholesomeTomatoTips.com

Now all you need to do is go over to yet another free and helpful tool on the Web, which is a bulk domain-name availability checker. Because these tools also change frequently, just go to www.sixfiguresecondincome.com and type the word "bulk" into the search box.

All you need to do is highlight all those 196 terms in the first tool, copy them, and then paste them into the second tool. In another couple of seconds you will have a list of all the domain names and which ones are available.

I hope you see why it's not necessary to include silly terms like "u" and "4" for "you" and "for." With just a small amount of creativity and a couple of online tools, you can find many great domain names that are available.

Warning: You May Become a Domain-Name Junkie this Way!

Don't say I didn't warn you. As an Opportunity Engineer, not only will you see opportunity and potential products everywhere, but you'll see lousy domain names and think *I can do better than that!* You'll go home, run these tools, and—sure enough—you were able to do better. You will then want to reserve some of the best names.

Pretty soon you'll own lots of domain names. The process of monetizing domain names is a whole separate discipline and some people get rich doing it. They either sell their good names to businesses that want them or they build specialized sites that earn them money for each name. This process is beyond the scope of the book, but I bring it up because, once you're a domain-name junkie, you may be able to make money from your odd habit.

Question: "Once I pick a great name for my info product is it important to get all the other versions of the same name, such as ".net," ".tv," ".info," and so on?"

Answer: I would not bother with those at the outset of your info-product promotion. Remember that you should be putting the least time into a project as you can during the early stages— I'm not saying you should do a shoddy job but I am saying you shouldn't yet build the *Taj Mahal*. First determine how popular your product becomes. At the earliest sign of it taking off you can reserve some of those other names.

The risk of doing it initially is that you'll quickly multiply your cost. You will spend about $10 per year to reserve your ".com" name. To get all the other versions you could spend $50 to $100 or more per year in total. It's a relatively unnecessary expense and you'll make more overall profit by taking that $100 and reserving many other great names for other great products you'll soon have on the drawing board.

Question: "What is a *private registration* and should I get it?"

Answer: The *domain registrar* where you reserve your names—companies like *GoDaddy* and *Network Solutions*—will strongly suggest that you get a private registration. It's a way of obscuring to the outside world the fact that you are the true owner of the domain name. They'll tell you that it's a form of protection for your name.

Don't bother. It's a great gimmick for those companies to increase their domain-name-related revenues, but it really doesn't protect you in any meaningful way. I've tried it and it's more of a pain and an expense than anything.

Question: "Which domain registrar should I use?"

Answer: I like GoDaddy.com. They have very good customer support, but you won't need it often because their system is straightforward. They also remind you when your annual renewals are coming up for domain names.

 Building Block Two: You Need to Arrange for Web Site Hosting

In a sense the World Wide Web is nothing more than millions of computers of all shapes and sizes hooked together with certain specific requirements.

Think of our system of roadways. You have your own driveway leading to your house. Within reason, you are the owner and controller of your driveway, which might be beautifully paved or it might be a dirt road.

As you head away from your house onto ever-larger roads, things begin to look more standardized. The city roads are wider than your driveway and the state highways are wider still. Finally, you get to the interstate roads, which are big and wide, with standardized signage and ramps.

Well, your home or office computer is like your home driveway. But your new web site needs the services of a specialized computer—a hosting service— that's part of that interstate system known as the World Wide Web.

Web hosting services are special computers first because they must be kept on 24 hours per day, every day of the year. The governing body for the Web insists that domain names follow certain standardized rules and one of them is you can't just have your domain name reachable when you feel like it, turning it off when you're on vacation.

You have great control over your *web site* but less control over your *domain name*. I don't want to get too detailed and confusing here, so I'll just get to the bottom line, which is that you need separate web hosting no matter how many computers you have at home and how good you are at using them.

Here's the good news about web hosting: Many companies will have you believe that you must pay $49 per month, $99 per month, or even more for web hosting. That's utter nonsense, because for only $3 per month you can get perfectly good hosting to start your business.

In fact, I've made millions of dollars of profits from web sites hosted at $3 per month. At one company I use, the customer service is so fast that if you send a question and get up to go to the bathroom you can expect that the answer will be waiting for you when you return.

As usual, Internet-related companies change so frequently that I don't want to print their names in this book, so for my latest recommendation just go to www .sixfiguresecondincome.com and type "hosting" into the search box.

Warning: Avoid Free Hosting Services

Some of the best things in life are free, but hosting ain't one of them. You can find plenty of free-hosting services on the Web, but almost all come with gimmicks, the biggest of which is they will use your site to advertise themselves or other services. Your site should only contain your stuff and no forced advertising for others.

Another scam with free hosting is they will often tell you: "Wait—there's more! With your free hosting account you'll get a free domain name! How sweet is that!"

It's not sweet at all. One problem is they may makc you have a name that you cannot choose but that's stuck inside a long string of letters like: www.organictomatosecrets.abc-xyzhostingservices.com. The worse problem is you might have the name you choose but they will own it. So when you eventually grow out of the cheapo free hosting service and want something good, just try to get them to give you your name back. They'll say, "Mr. Jones, you agreed to our Terms of Service for our free hosting account and part of that contract fine print is that ABCXYZ Hosting Services owns the name you chose. Now we are reasonable people and if you would like to purchase your name from us, we're willing to sell it to you. . . ." They know they have you over a barrel because you did agree to all those pages of fine print.

There's only one exception I can think of to the free-hosting gimmicks out there. Google actually has a service where you can get a free site hosted and maintained by Google itself. It's not a fancy site, but hey, the price is right. In certain situations it may be all you need. If you would like more information on this service go to www.sixfiguresecondincome.com and type "Google hosting" into the search box.

Question: "Is web hosting the same as my web site? Where does my web site actually reside?"

Answer: Your web site is just an account at a web hosting company. You'll open the account and they will give you instructions on how to set up your web pages on their computers. You might have a copy of your web site on your own home computer, but the *official* copy is on the hosting company computers.

Question: "But my Uncle Louie swears that his genius kid Melvin can do anything with computers and Melvin once told me he could host any site I wanted for free right from his home computer."

Answer: If good hosting is three bucks a month, why would you want to hope that Melvin knows what he's talking about? Besides, we all hear about *cyber attacks* practically daily, where hackers in Asia, Eastern Europe, or the high school down the street have managed to breach the security at a large company.

Hackers are indeed a real problem. Therefore, you need a web hosting company that's staffed with full-time security professionals whose only job is to monitor the computers for hacker attacks and repel them. A freebie site or Uncle Louie's kid are not adequate safeguards against these troublemakers.

Speaking of troublemakers, here's a bit of advanced advice. Once you are up and running with a few web sites and you see a steady stream of income, consider getting what's called *dedicated IP hosting*.

Every computer has an *Internet Protocol Address*, or *IP address* for short. The vast majority of hosting services put hundreds of their customers' web sites on a single powerful computer, with the result that those customers share the same IP address.

Let's assume for a minute that your hosting company put 280 different customer web sites on one of its computers. Let's further assume that—contrary to the policies of the hosting company—a few of those customers decided to put up pornography sites or sites that send lots of spam about Viagra®.

If that happens, sometimes Google and other search engines will *blacklist* that IP address. The result is the bad guys—and the other 270+ sites on that same computer—are now banned, and you will not show up in the Google listings. They can taint your reputation for something entirely out of your control.

Hosting companies are getting better at catching that kind of activity and it's possible to appeal to Google when innocent bystanders are affected, but that can take time. Therefore, it's a good practice to get dedicated IP hosting, where you are the only web site on a fresh, pristine IP address. You can even choose to have all of your sites on the same single address, but that's okay because all your sites will be good, nonspammy ones.

Dedicated IP hosting costs a few more dollars than shared IP hosting—it's more like $30 per month for the first web site and around $1 per month for any additional sites you host. If you'd like my current recommendation for dedicated IP hosting just go to www.sixfiguresecondincome.com and type "dedicated IP" into the search box.

Question: "If dedicated IP hosting is better, then why wouldn't I want to get it from the outset? Why should I wait?"

Answer: I'm just trying to get you a good site for the lowest cost and with only manageable risks. If you're extremely short on cash, then go the $3-per-month route until your info-product business starts to bring in money. I would hate for you to pay more for hosting and watch the expenses add up, only to bag the whole idea of a six-figure second income before you see the money coming in. Right now, do what you can afford.

 Building Block Three: Get a Web Site Design

If your web hosting is working properly it will be invisible to anyone visiting your site. Now let's tackle the issue of what your site will look like to anyone who types in your web address.

One thing that deters people from ever creating a web site is the thought that they're not programmers or graphic designers. Fortunately, you can have a great web site without knowing much at all about programming or graphic design.

Let's look at your options for designing a web site.

Option One: Custom-Programmed from the Ground Up

This is really unnecessary. If you were a large corporation then you might want everything custom-built for you because nothing off-the-shelf seems to fit your needs. When you get to the point of being a large corporation then you can ponder this option, which is also usually more expensive than the alternatives.

I say *usually more expensive* because it's becoming more practical to have a site custom-coded for you. Remember in the last chapter I talked about the web site www.99designs

.com and how you can get a T-shirt design created? You can also sponsor a contest to have a whole web site design created for you for a few hundred bucks.

The contestants will submit designs only, not the programming necessary to make all the web-page menus work or have all the buttons clickable. Once you pick your winning design, you can have that design turned into an actual, usable web site with all the programming, also known as *coding*, done for you. Just go to www.sixfiguresecond income.com and type "design coding" into the search box and I'll tell you my current favorite source for this service.

Even though what I just described is a nice option, you're really paying more than you need to pay for a perfectly workable web site. I'd only suggest that route if you have your heart set on a specific design or set of features and you simply can't find it anywhere else.

Option Two: Learn Programming and Build it Yourself

Ouch. Hey, if you enjoy that kind of activity then by all means learn the programming languages of HTML, CSS, PHP, JavaScript, and others necessary to create a solid site.

Only do it if you enjoy it, though, because otherwise it's not the best use of your time. The days and weeks you spend learning those skills could be better spent creating another info product.

I do agree that knowing something about programming is a good thing because you're less likely to be intimidated by a programmer who gives you a song-and-dance about how a task will take really long to complete. Even then it's possible to ask your buddies in your soon-to-be-large network of info-marketer friends and they'll quickly let you know if your programmer is telling the truth.

In terms of cost, this option is effectively free. The tools to learn programming are available free on the web. Simply

Google a term like "learn web programming" and you'll see a ton of them.

Option Three: Use a Wizard–Based System

Some companies have web-based online *wizards* that lead you through a series of questions and screens at the end of which you have a web site designed and ready to go. Until recently these systems were great in theory but in reality they required you to learn their own involved procedures for changing web pages. Every year or so a new generation of these tools comes on the scene and current systems are becoming more intuitive.

This option has another problem relating to customization. These companies are great if all you want to do is take one of their hundreds of pretty designs and stick your text on the page. However, if you want a slightly different page—for instance, you'd like to add a box here or eliminate a photo from the top of the page—they'll tell you, "Sorry, that's not going to be possible."

These systems are often bundled with web hosting and domain names for a real one-stop-shopping experience. Occasionally, they play games with who owns the domain name and they definitely will charge you more than a few dollars per month for hosting. Still, it's relatively inexpensive.

I'm constantly on the lookout for wizard-based systems that combine ease of use with enough custom capabilities. If you want to know if I have any current favorites in this category simply go to www.sixfiguresecondincome.com and type "wizard system" into the search box.

Option Four: Use an Off-the-Shelf Template

This is how I've done the majority of my web sites. A template is an entire web site that contains all of the professionally created design and programming, but it has placeholders for text and graphics. You then add your own pictures, text, links, and whatever else you want.

It differs from the wizard-based system because with a template you can customize anything. Some templates allow you to move many elements around on the page without knowing programming by instead employing a drag-and-drop approach.

It comes down to knowing what you want to accomplish with a site. If all you want to do is stick your text and pictures into the template, then you might as well go the wizard route. The template-based approach requires a bit more knowledge on your part in exchange for lots more flexibility.

Another option with templates is to hire a programmer to do the customization for you. It's usually a pretty inexpensive proposition, measured in tens of dollars to perhaps a few hundred dollars.

Templates are also quite inexpensive. They range from around $20 for a simple one to maybe $150 for a very sophisticated one. If you want to know my current favorites in this category simply go to www.sixfiguresecondincome .com and type "template" into the search box.

Question: "I'm really starting from scratch here and don't trust myself to learn much web-related stuff. I can afford to pay a little bit but have to watch my dollars pretty carefully. What would you recommend?"

Answer: In that case your best bet is to start with Option Three—the wizard-based system. It will get you up and running the quickest, and that should mean that profits are coming back to you the quickest. That will give you the luxury of sitting back and deciding how you would like to improve your site. If the wizard system can accommodate those improvements, then great. If it cannot, then you'll know what specific modifications you want to make to your current site and you can move either to the template approach—Option Four— or to more of a custom site.

If you do decide to go with Option Three, the good news is you can skip the next two Building Blocks and go right to Building Block Six. However, you might want to breeze through these next two blocks just so you know what they contain.

Building Block Four: Get an HTML Editor

The granddaddy language of the World Wide Web is HTML, or *hypertext markup language*. At one time almost all web pages were constructed using that language, which dictates where text and images will appear on the page and how they will look. Even today most web pages contain some HTML despite other languages gaining in popularity.

As I said before, you'll never need to become a programmer in order to make a great deal of money with info products. In fact, you'll hear a number of other info-marketing gurus trumpet: "I don't know the first thing about computers and look at all the money I've made!"

I think that's going a little overboard. It's like a person being so helpless that he's somehow proud to say, "I can't even turn on a washing machine. I've always had people to do my laundry for me."

Personally, I like to be just a little bit self-sufficient and not totally held hostage to techie people for the least little change to a web site. It's handy, for instance, to be able to change an address or a date on a web page without submitting a request to someone and waiting for it to happen.

Also, as you'll read in a later chapter, most search engines focus on certain elements of HTML in order to determine the quality and nature of a web page. Therefore an informal knowledge of HTML is helpful.

You can get a very good HTML editing tool for free. I'll give you the current location of it when you go to www.sixfiguresecondincome.com and type the term "HTML" in the search box.

The tool works in a similar fashion to a word processor. If you bought a template for your web-page design, you can open that page in the HTML editor. On part of your computer screen you'll see the web page and on another part you'll see the programming language mixed in with the text that shows up on the web page. When you change the text that relates to a date, for instance, then you'll see that date instantly change on the web page on your desktop. You then can click a few buttons and have that new page sent to your web host to put on your live site.

I would measure the learning curve to be a few hours over one weekend in order to have a basic understanding of HTML. It may be a fair trade of your time, considering how it will give you a greater understanding of web sites and search engines.

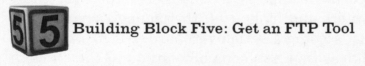 **Building Block Five: Get an FTP Tool**

The term *FTP* stands for *File Transfer Protocol*. Sooner or later you'll hear this term in the world of web sites because it's the main way for web pages, audio files, and other documents to get from your desktop to your web host and then onto your web site.

For instance, let's say you just finished recording an interview and the audio file is rather large. You most likely cannot send it to someone by attaching it to an e-mail. Most e-mail systems choke with large files and, even if yours does not, there's a good chance your recipient's e-mail may reject the message as being too large.

A tool known as an *FTP client* will save the day and allow you to send huge files over the Internet. The term *client* in this context means the same as *tool that sits on your computer*.

If you go the template route to build your web site, you'll definitely need an FTP client. They're inexpensive—a one-time fee of about $40, a learning curve of about 10 minutes, and you'll use it for years.

I'll give you my current FTP tool recommendation when you go to www.sixfiguresecondincome.com and type the term "FTP" in the search box.

6 6 Building Block Six: Learn How to Accept Money on the Web

That's what it's all about, right? Of course, money isn't everything, but you did buy this book so it could show you how to make a six-figure second income.

PayPal
The easiest and fastest way to allow people to pay you over the Web is to get a *PayPal* account. The PayPal service is owned by eBay, which you probably know is a Web powerhouse. That means most customers either already do business on eBay and are accustomed to PayPal, or they've at least heard the name.

From the customers' perspective, paying via PayPal is not really different from paying any other way on the web.

They do not need to open a PayPal account but instead can use their credit or debit cards to buy your product or service. They also are not charged a fee for doing so. On the other hand, PayPal does want to get paid for the service so it takes a few percent of the customers' funds before forwarding the rest onto you.

Opening a PayPal account is very quick and easy. Simply go to www.paypal.com and follow the instructions. After the initial setup you'll be asked for your bank account number. PayPal will then make two deposits of literally pennies each and will ask you to go to your bank account and find those deposit amounts. When you then enter those specific penny amounts on the screen back at PayPal, you've just verified that you have access to the bank account and didn't simply make up a fictional account.

I won't go into all the *whys* and *hows* of PayPal, but suffice it to say that it's a great service for info marketers. Without opening any new bank accounts or going through a bunch of red tape you can almost immediately take credit-card payments over the web.

You are in for a great treat the first time you get a message from PayPal stating that someone bought your product and your PayPal balance has gone up by that amount. It's even better when the money comes in while you were sleeping because it reinforces the point that this business can make you money around the clock if you set it up right.

Despite the fact that PayPal wanted to know your bank account number, PayPal keeps those payments to you in a separate account it maintains so, if customers pay you, PayPal increases your balance. If customers send back your product and request a refund, PayPal deducts that amount from your balance.

PayPal will even issue you a debit card if you want one, so you can go shopping with the PayPal MasterCard and buy whatever you want with the money in your PayPal account. This brings me to a very important—and little understood—aspect of PayPal: Many of your future customers regard their PayPal balances as *funny money*.

Let's say you set up an eBay account, sold a number of things around the house, and now have $233.15 in your PayPal account. Because that money did not come via a paycheck, it takes on more of an *easy come, easy go* appearance than does your bank account balance. It's almost like finding a $10 bill on the ground or having a bookstore tell you that you have $20 to spend any way you want in the store—you don't tend to agonize over the purchases with this money in the same way as the money you earned at work.

That funny-money aspect of PayPal is great news for you and me as merchants because it lowers the resistance to buying our products when we accept PayPal as a means of payment.

Checks and Money Orders
It's even easier for you to accept checks and money orders on your web site than it is to open a quick PayPal account. You only need to state on your web site that you accept checks and money orders. Then tell customers to whom to make out the check or money order and where to send it. Once you receive the payment and wait for it to clear, you will ship the goods.

Even in our twenty-first century cyber age it's still a good policy to accept checks and money orders. Many people are wary of entering their credit card numbers over the web, despite all the mechanisms in place to encrypt that information.

Maybe they've been the victims of identity theft in the past or maybe they're just old school—either way, their money is still good and they want your product. It's worth allowing them to send you money in the mode they're most comfortable with.

Question: "Should I have the option on my site for people to send cash?"

Answer: I would not recommend it. At least with checks and money orders you have a paper trail of the transaction, but with cash, you could potentially get into a situation where someone swears he sent you cash and you swear you never received it.

Taking Credit Cards and Debit Cards Directly

When I say *directly* I mean the ability to accept cards right on your site and not through the PayPal service.

Sooner or later you'll want to have this feature because it gives you more flexibility. Not only does the money flow directly into your own bank account but you also have more options concerning what customers see when they check out. In contrast, once they're taken to the PayPal site your options are limited for adding language to reinforce the sale.

I still strongly recommend that you get PayPal set up as your first payment-acceptance option. That will give you the luxury of immediately being able to accept money on your site while you work out the process of taking credit cards directly.

And it is indeed a process. Let's go through each step.

Step One: Get a Business Certificate. Typically, the road to having an officially recognized business starts at your local city hall. States differ on this process so you should of course Google terms like *starting a business in Iowa* to determine your current rules.

Cities like to know what sort of businesses are being set up within their jurisdiction and they also like to collect fees. You'll fill out a page or two of questions asking whether you're building a factory, raising pigs, or engaging in other forms of commerce. I can guarantee you that they will not have a box for *Information Product Creator*. The closest match you're likely to find is *Publishing* or perhaps *Other*. When they realize that your business will not be causing traffic jams or toxic waste—and when your check clears—you'll be good to go.

Question: "Should I set up a corporation?"

Answer: I'm not an attorney or a tax advisor and you should check with the people you trust to give you legal and tax advice, okay? But if you want my opinion as a private citizen, you probably should not set up a corporation before creating your first info product. I'm presuming that your info product is not about a new way to rig a parachute or great ways to mix chemicals found in your garage so that they cure cancer. I assume your first product is something nice and safe like *Yes You Can Plan Your Wedding Faster and Cheaper than They Tell You* or *Dog Grooming Secrets the Pros Haven't Told You About—Until Now*.

If I'm correct about the kind of product you'll create then you won't expose yourself to much liability. Also, corporations can run into many hundreds of dollars or even more of set-up costs. I'm all for enjoying the tax benefits and protection that corporations provide, but you might start the flow of money toward you first, and then get one set up soon afterward.

Besides, you need to discuss with a good advisor whether the best structure for you is a *Subchapter S corporation*, a *C corporation*, a *limited liability company*, or some other option.

Step Two: Get a Commercial Bank Account. With the ink still drying on your business certificate you can go down to your favorite bank and open a commercial bank account. It's pretty much the same as a personal bank account except they'll ask you for your company name, and you're required to have one. When picking a name it's a good idea to see if a matching domain name is available and to reserve it. Otherwise, you could run into trouble when someone else already owns your company name.

Step Three: Get a Merchant Account. These are special companies whose whole business is to be an interface between commercial bank accounts, like your new one, and all the credit card companies, like MasterCard, Visa, American Express, and so on.

The merchant account is not a bank account but instead a set of agreements between many parties. You must tell the merchant account provider the nature of your business like information publishing, hair salon, online gambling service, or whatever. The provider will only allow you to accept credit cards for the activities you list. Therefore, if you're approved for a merchant account for information publishing, then you cannot accept a credit card as payment for that new type of lawnmower you now want to sell.

The merchant account agreement will also require you to keep customers' credit card numbers in a safe place, promptly process refunds when customers are eligible for refunds, and abide by many other rules. It's a lengthy contract, but you better read it because these people are serious about your following the rules. It's just part of doing business as a full-fledged merchant that can accept credit cards.

In exchange for all of those requirements you meet, the credit card companies and merchant account provider agree to process your customers' cards promptly, send you notices for each sale, and help to resolve disputes when some customers may claim that they never ordered your product.

Step Four: Get a Payment Gateway. You may have heard of merchant accounts before but chances are good that you've never heard of payment gateways, yet they're critical to your ability to take credit cards directly.

A payment gateway is all the computer connections between you, your bank account, and the credit card companies, just as the merchant account is all the agreements between those parties.

When your customers hit the Buy Now button on your web site, the payment gateway swings into action and first validates the credit card number and expiration date.

Then the gateway validates the customer's address. This is an important step to prevent credit card fraud. Let's say Mary Jones lives at 123 Main Street in Chicago, but now someone claiming to be Mary Jones is trying to buy your product and the buyer enters on your web site a billing address of 456 South Avenue instead of 123 Main Street. If that credit card was stolen the thief may not know the correct billing address. The payment gateway performs this address verification check and gets either a green light and continues to process the transaction or a red light, in which case you—the merchant—will receive an e-mail that the transaction was attempted but it failed due to an address mismatch.

Assuming the address is fine the payment gateway then checks for sufficient funds in the customer's bank account. If the customer doesn't have sufficient funds then the transaction won't go through and all parties get notified of that. If the customer has sufficient funds then all parties get notified and the funds are transferred from the customer's account to yours. All of this happens in a fraction of a second.

As we discussed, some customers will not want to enter their credit card numbers on the Web but will prefer to give you the card details over the phone. In that case you'll be able to log into your payment gateway and enter the card details for the customers. You'll get instant notification if the transaction was successful or not.

Step Five: Get a Shopping Cart.   Now that you have all the behind-the-scenes accounts and tools set up, they come together in the form of a shopping cart on your web site.

The shopping cart software allows customers to specify first the quantity of products they want to buy and then to put one or more products into their online virtual cart. When customers are ready to check out, they're taken to a special secure, encrypted page where they enter their credit card details. Typically, your web browser will show a little padlock somewhere on the screen to indicate that the web page you're on is secure.

Some merchants are lazy and don't bother with the secure-page part. That is not only a good way to get in hot water with the credit card companies, but many customers look for the little padlock icon on the screen and will not enter their credit card details without it. That results in lost sales because many of those customers will not bother to pick up the phone and call the merchant with their card details. You should regularly check your web site to make sure it's showing the padlock icon and everything is running smoothly—no *Page Not Found* errors and so on.

The cart also calculates state sales tax and enables customers to specify the type of shipping they'd like. When customers hit the PAY NOW button the shopping cart interfaces with the payment gateway to perform all the checks and authorizations.

Customers will next see a screen that either tells them the transaction was successful or it indicates the nature of any problem. In the case of downloadable products the cart will allow the customer to download the product from a special page after paying for it.

I cannot overemphasize the importance of having a good shopping cart. Everything you've done up to this point as an info marketer has been to get the customers to take out their credit cards and enter them on your site. This is not the time to blow the transaction with confusing instructions, hard-to-read text, unclear policies, or software that hiccups and does not smoothly handle the transactions.

You know what I'm talking about because you as a consumer have been the victim of these types of poor shopping carts before. A good cart is constructed so the checkout and payment procedures are smooth and confidence-building for the customers.

Another excellent aspect of the better shopping carts is they allow you to offer an additional product or service to customers who just that moment finished buying your first product. This is known as an *upsell*. The most famous example of an upsell is when you order a burger at McDonald's and the person asks: "Would you like fries with that?" You're free to say "no thanks," but McDonald's knows from countless millions of customers that a certain number of people will think, *"Hey sure, why not?"* and order the fries on impulse.

Of course, some companies carry this process to an extreme and pester customers with too many upsell attempts, one after another. If you do it right, though, you're offering a complementary service to customers at the very moment they have their credit cards out and are in a buying mood. It's an extremely effective method of marketing.

Good shopping cart software also allows you to run all sorts of reports on your customers—who bought what, when did the buy, which products are most popular, what patterns exist for popularity of product by region of the country, and so on.

If you would like my current recommendations for merchant accounts, payment gateways, and shopping carts just go to www.sixfiguresecondincome.com and type the words "direct cards" into the search box.

All this stuff is a decent amount of work but I have good news for you—once it's set up you really don't have to deal with it again. You may change the shipping preferences you want to offer your clients or make other small adjustments, but once set up the system will pretty much run on autopilot.

 Building Block Seven: Set Up an Effective E–Mail System

"Oh, I have e-mail already so I can skip this section." That would be a big mistake, because *having e-mail* as a private citizen and *having e-mail* as an information marketer are two very different beasts. In a later chapter I will discuss the content you need to have in your e-mails in order to make the most money, but right now let's talk about the system you must put into place.

Home E-Mail Accounts

The chances are good that you have had a Hotmail, AOL, Comcast, or similar e-mail account at some point. When you sign up for home Internet service your vendor—also known as an *Internet Service Provider* or *ISP* for short—will give you home e-mail accounts.

And they do mean *home account*, because they get very cranky when you start to send lots of commercial e-mail from your home account. How do they know it's commercial e-mail? They can detect commercial e-mail in two ways.

First, the ISPs scan your outgoing e-mails for certain words that tell them you are sending commercial e-mail. It's not a certainty but a statistical probability that if your e-mail uses combinations of *stop words* like *free*, *buy*, *product*, *guarantee*, *cost*, *payment*, *discount*, and hundreds of other words, you're probably not talking to Grandma but to a potential customer.

Note: Don't just try to avoid the few words I mention above because the list contains hundreds of words, and it varies from ISP to ISP. The bottom line is they know when you're sending a nonpersonal e-mail.

Second, the ISPs monitor if you send a single e-mail to one person or that same e-mail to many dozens, hundreds, or thousands of people all at once. Their systems light up like a Christmas tree if you not only have those *stop words* in your e-mail, but you're also sending the exact same text to even just a dozen people in short order.

The least-bad thing that will happen to you if you send that sort of e-mail is it will reach your ISP's red-flag system but they will not allow it to leave their servers and be sent to the recipient addresses. They may or may not even tell you that they refused to send the mail, by the way.

The next bad thing that can happen is your ISP will not allow you to send e-mails at all, or they may boot you off the e-mail system entirely.

It gets worse. Even if you somehow manage to get the e-mails through, you'll encounter another whole set of e-mail filters on the other end—the recipient end. Therefore, if Comcast, for instance, notices that suddenly hundreds of its customers are receiving the exact same e-mail with all those same *stop words* in each e-mail, they might either delay or reject those e-mails from all of the Comcast e-mail accounts. If they're feeling particularly frisky they will ban *any of your future e-mails* from ever reaching any Comcast accounts! They won't even bother to tell you but suddenly none of your Comcast customers has heard a peep from you, nor will they ever again.

I use Comcast as an example but most of the other big ISPs like AOL, Hotmail, and Gmail work the same way.

Question: "But Uncle Louie's kid Melvin told me he can hook me up with software that's specifically designed for businesses. It only costs a one-time fee and it will completely automate the process of sending and receiving business e-mail. Why do I need to go to some separate company to handle my e-mail?"

Answer: Would you quit listening to Uncle Louie and his kid Melvin already? The reason they're not rich is they either shoot down other people's ambitions or they look for cheapo shortcuts to doing the job right. The type of software they're talking about does sit on your desktop and does manage all the outgoing and incoming e-mail—but it does so by using your same home e-mail account. Therefore, all that software will do is automate and quicken the pain you'll feel when the sending ISP or the receiving ISPs cut you off at the knees.

Commercial E-Mail Accounts

What's the solution to this mess? It's to get a commercial e-mail account. A whole industry has sprung up in recent years whose only purpose is to handle the delivery of commercial e-mail from companies to their intended recipients.

The purpose of a commercial e-mail account is to get legitimate business e-mail to its intended recipients and filter out everything else. Your commercial account will test your e-mail message for you and give you a score of how spammy it is, and therefore its likelihood of being red-flagged.

You will simply not believe the sophisticated systems in use today to detect spam e-mail. It's become a real cat-and-mouse game. Years ago the systems created those stop words like free, guarantee, and so on. Then spammers started to get cute and send messages with words like *fr.ee* because spammers know that humans can read *fr.ee* as *free* but machines may think it's a new, innocent word.

That was effective for a few months of sending spam until the filters got more sophisticated so now they're on to that little ploy about mis-spelling words on purpose. I highly recommend that you not play games like that, not only because they'll most likely not work, but because they also make you look like a spammer.

The competition is fierce between commercial e-mail account providers. As a result, many of them will allow you to have a free account as long as you have only a few hundred customer e-mail names and you don't send massive amounts of e-mail. The only negative with some of these free accounts is they will attach to the bottom of your outgoing e-mails a small promotion for their service. That's a small price to pay for a good service that actually gets your e-mails delivered. Besides, you can always upgrade to a paid account when your list size and profits grow.

Warning: All Commercial E-Mail Vendors Are Not Created Equal!

As crazy as it sounds, the very best vendors are sometimes the most difficult to deal with.

Think about it for a minute: The way good commercial e-mail vendors work is they painstakingly cultivate a great reputation with the ISPs like Comcast, AOL, Hotmail, and the others. They build that reputation by making sure that, if an e-mail is sent from that commercial e-mail vendor, those ISPs can relax and know it was a quality message and not something related to *Discount Vi@Gr@ pills!!!*

The e-mail vendor must therefore become the tough guy, and the very best ones are really tough. They will monitor the type of e-mail you send very closely—and that's only after you have passed an application process. If they see any irregularities with your e-mails or the way they were perceived by the recipients, they'll contact you and insist on an explanation.

I know it sounds like a lot of work, but the alternative is to think you successfully sent, say, 2,000 e-mails only to have the vast majority of them never reach your customers' inboxes. You might even change your marketing approach because you concluded that customers didn't like your message when in reality they never saw it.

Look at the bright side: When you work with a tough e-mail vendor your e-mails will get through and all the spammy garbage your competitors may want to send will never see the light of day.

The other good news is, when you send quality e-mails with good information, it tends to sail right through the spam filters. You still need the commercial account, though, because, if you follow the steps in this book, you'll eventually send a great deal of e-mail and only commercial accounts can handle the volume effectively.

For the names of commercial e-mail vendors I currently recommend, go to www.sixfiguresecondincome.com and type "e-mail" in the search box.

Another Benefit: You Can Name Your Own E-Mail Accounts

Speaking of e-mail accounts, when you reserve that new domain name you'll have the ability to create your own e-mail accounts. For instance, if you reserved BestBass FishingSecrets.com then you are free to create as many different e-mail addresses as you want: Bubba@BestBass FishingSecrets.com, Questions@BestBassFishingSecrets.com, and so on. In a matter of two or three minutes you can set up a new account—that is, a new name like "bonus@ . . ."—through your web-hosting provider. Then you can easily have that e-mail forwarded wherever you like.

For example, let's say you set up a new e-mail of Bubba@ BestBassFishingSecrets.com and you don't want to have to check every day whether new mail came to that address. On the web site control panel, which your web host will give you access to, you'll be able to specify which e-mail address should receive any of the mail from that new address you set up. It will be automatically forwarded to you, and you'll be able to see that it was originally sent to the "Bubba@" address.

Handling E-Mail on Your Web Site

There are two ways to set up your web site to receive communications from visitors—a lazy way and a correct way.

The lazy way is to use what's known as a *mailto:* link. Web pages are built to recognize the word *mailto:*, so if I create text on the web page that says mailto:bob@xyz.com then when the web visitor clicks on that text with *mailto:* in it, the visitor's own e-mail account will start up and stick bob@xyz.com in the address to send that e-mail.

Here's the problem: At any given time a high percentage of web visitors have problems with their own e-mail accounts, whether they be through Comcast, AOL, Hotmail, or whomever. If your web site is now relying on the visitors' e-mail accounts to work in order to send that e-mail, you've now blown a hole in the amount of communication you'll receive from visitors.

The correct way to have visitors contact you on your site is through the use of a *web form*. You've seen them—they're the forms with little boxes to fill in your name and message and they usually have a gray *Submit* button at the bottom.

When visitors use that type of form, the message travels right from your web site to you without ever relying on the visitors' own e-mail systems to deliver it. Any web site design template you buy will have those forms already made and ready for you to customize with where you want the visitor messages to be sent.

GETTING WORK DONE FOR YOU

This has been a long chapter filled with many details about getting your business up and running on the web. It may seem like a lot of work, but it's simply putting one foot in front of the other. No one step is a giant leap. Besides, I've given you a number of options to consider so the actual process you'll choose has fewer moving parts than all the variations we've discussed.

Also keep in mind that, once you set up these tools and procedures, they'll be behind you. Your first info product will take a certain amount of time to set up, but the second, third, and subsequent info products will each take a tiny fraction of that time because you'll be able simply to clone and modify everything you did for the first info product.

As soon as practical you should consider outsourcing some of the work to others. Initially, you may not have the resources to hire anyone, so you might do the work yourself. But you'll be very smart if you plow some of your early revenues back into building a team of people who can take the drudgery off your shoulders.

Let's say your first info product is SchnauzerGrooming Secrets.com and you've had so much success that you quickly want to come out with PoodleGroomingSecrets .com. Don't even think about having a site with both Schnauzer and Poodle grooming information! Those dog owners love their breeds in a special way and only want to see information about their one particular breed.

What you should do is outsource the work to set up the new web site, change around the pages to incorporate Poodle pictures, and so on. I've already told you about www.99designs.com for web designers and other special-ists. You should also check out www.elance.com, www .rentacoder.com, and www.odesk.com. They are all good sources for temporary technical help.

The way most of them work is they are split into two sections—one for people looking for work and the other for people looking to hire specialists. Typically, you can browse around the site anonymously.

When you get serious about finding someone to help you, first you register at the site so they have your name and contact information. Then you post a project outline, where you should be as explicit and detailed as you can. For instance, you might say that you're the owner of Schnauzer GroomingSecrets.com and you want to create another site along those lines, and how it must be five pages with certain changes you have in mind. You spell out every detail in the project description.

If you're skittish about revealing the nature of the new project, you have some options. You can either create a private project so the whole world won't see the project but only actual candidates can see it, or you can simply be specific about the page details but vague about the actual topic.

Let's say you work through Elance.com and you set the budget for your project at $150. You'll then post the $150 to an escrow account controlled by Elance.com. Escrow accounts are for the protection of all parties. On the one hand you don't want to be a programmer who builds a bunch of pages and sends them to the customer who never gets around to paying you. On the other hand you don't want to pay a programmer to do work but he never quite finishes the project after he's paid.

When Elance.com holds the escrow money it gets agreement from both parties that the work was done before the money moves from the escrow account to the programmer. If the programmer never completed the work then Elance.com will return the escrow money to you. Elance.com also acts as an intermediary in any disputes, which can happen when one party is vague and the other party misunderstands the instructions. That's all the more reason to be highly specific when you hire someone to help you.

Before you initiate a project on one of these sites, spend some time looking at all the people who offer their services and review the portfolios of work they've done for other clients. I think you'll be impressed with the excellent work some freelancers do.

You need to get a sense of how to narrow your specifications for people you'll hire. For instance, will you accept only workers from the United States or is Europe also okay but not Asia? Maybe you only want people who are rated at least four stars out of five stars. Maybe you insist that they've passed certain proficiency tests that Elance.com and the others offer. You may even prefer to work with people of a certain gender or of a certain age range.

I can't answer those questions for you because they depend on the supply/demand equation for the project you have. Basic web programming is a very popular area and you can literally find thousands of potential specialists to do the work. On the other hand you may want to use that Joomla program I spoke of in the last chapter and hook it up to the special XYZ e-mail system, in which case you've just narrowed the field of candidates considerably.

Don't give up too soon on this process. All you need to find is a handful of great people who can work with you on project after project. It's worth going through a number of candidates to find those gems.

Also be very wary of going with some of the amazingly low prices you'll be quoted by some people. I've had projects where literally 10 minutes after I posted the project there were bidders, some of whom would say they'd do the job for $5 or even $3 when others wanted $50 to $150 for the same project. I'm sure that a few people in poor countries are so desperate for work that they might even do a decent job for $3, but sometimes I just get a good or bad gut feeling about the candidate.

My gut feeling deteriorates when I get an instant response from a candidate who doesn't even refer to my specific project but sends me a canned message like "We do great and fast workings! You can count your business on us to deliver well."

On the other hand, my gut feeling about a candidate is improved when I read glowing comments from many past clients. I've even had a few candidates really impress me by doing the work instantly and posting it to the project area—without my even hiring them yet! They're so fast and confident in their work that they complete the task while other candidates continue to ask me for clarification and needless details.

One excellent approach is to hire two people to do the very same task at the same time. You may initially think that is a waste of money because you only need the job done once. You can make it a relatively small task that's part of a larger project. The benefit of a side-by-side horse race is then you really have a basis by which you can judge these people against each other. Who completed the task faster? Who did a more thorough job? Who went above and beyond and actually exceeded your expectations?

Once you find such a person you'll have a valuable member of your team. Just be sure to treat him or her as a valuable member: Be specific in your requests, communicate promptly and in detail, leave good feedback about the person, and most definitely pay promptly.

I have found some great people all over the planet to help me with projects. Sometimes I even give them a bonus of another 10 percent or so of the project cost because their bid was very reasonable and their work was excellent. That's the way to cultivate team members who will drop what they're doing to take on your next project.

Are you getting excited about what you're discovering? Do you see how all those barriers to this business are helpful *Keep Out!* signs to the dabblers and the Uncle Moe's of the world, but that in reality the sky's the limit with this information-product business?

The next chapter is crucial to building your empire. It's all about how to get people to raise their hands with some level of interest in what you have to offer.

CHAPTER 5

How to Get People to Raise Their Hands

Are you confused about the best way to get prospects for your product or service? It's no wonder. If you've spent any time researching on the web the topic of *lead generation*, you've encountered the perfect storm of get-rich-quick hucksters teaming up with self-proclaimed gurus and programmer geeks who think they've stumbled onto the biggest, baddest, and best web game-changer gimmick ever.

Well, it's time to cut through all the nonsense and set you up with some solid reference points, kind of like lighthouses you can use to navigate through the storm to your profit destination.

This chapter is devoted not to getting customers, but to getting prospects or leads, which we'll later turn into customers. It's kind of like romance. If you ultimately want to get married to someone, you don't start with the topic of getting a spouse, but instead you first might want to get a date. In our present discussion, we will focus on *leads*.

Let's start by sweeping away several common and extremely dangerous myths about getting leads for your business.

MYTH NUMBER ONE: "IT'S ALL ABOUT TRAFFIC"

In the early days of the Web everyone talked about *hits*. "Hey, how many hits you got to your site today? I got

40,000!'' Marketers thought *hits* were a measure of how many people came to their site but in reality it was something different. If you had three pictures, two tables, and a form on a single web page, then that added up to six separate items that your web browser needed to load in order for you to see that page. So one person viewing that one page resulted in six hits.

After a while, knowledgeable people started to define *hits* as *How Idiots Track Success* because it became an arbitrary measure of volume but not of success.

Pretty soon the conversation changed to traffic: "It's all about traffic. . . . How do I get traffic. . . . I need more traffic!" At least this was an improvement over hits, because it measured human visitors and not items loading on a page.

Traffic is the easiest thing in the world to get. Simply go online to Google and search its image library for *bikini*. Now grab one of the pictures and stick it in an ad. Within minutes you will begin to see thousands of clicks on that picture to your web site. Young men all over the globe will have their tongues hanging out wanting to see more bikini pictures on your site.

Are you happy now that your traffic has shot through the roof? Maybe you are if you just want to brag to your buddies at the saloon that you had 1.3 million visitors to your site yesterday. However, your bank account is no better for it and might even be emptier, because your web host will either charge you for the extra traffic or shut you down.

Recently, the focus has shifted from traffic to *Facebook friends* or *Twitter followers*. This is just as absurd a measure as hits or traffic. A brilliant marketer by the name of Seth Godin was asked about the value of social networking and he said:

It's worthless to have lots of friends on Facebook because they're not really your friends. They're just people who didn't want to offend you by pressing the *Ignore* button. And if you have 5,000 people following you on Twitter because you tell a dirty joke every couple of hours that's not useful for your business, either.

The Internet is a giant cocktail party with all these people swarming around and keeping score — *Who likes me today? Who's talking about me today?* What matters is where are the real relationships. Networking is always important when it's real, and it's always a useless distraction when it's fake.

There's a reason why the book you're holding is not called *Six-Figure Traffic* and instead is called *The Six-Figure Second Income*. Your goal should be to get the income and profits you're after with the least amount of traffic you need to get there.

MYTH NUMBER TWO: "IT'S ALL ABOUT TARGETED TRAFFIC"

This is more of a half-truth than a myth, because I do agree that targeted traffic is great. The *myth* part is all in how you define *targeted*.

Most people define it way too broadly, again because their ego is tied to size. I suspect we males of the species have had a fixation with size for the last, oh, million years or so.

Let's say you want to publish an info product on *37 Secrets to Outfit Your Bass Boat to Win Competitions*. You wrote your report and followed all my advice about setting up your site. You see the futility of getting any old traffic to your site, but what about *fishermen*? What about *boat owners*?

Even those terms are way too broad. If you go after fishermen in general, you'll get people who love to go fly fishing in the mountains, plus big fans of surf-casting in the ocean, not to mention the lobster fishermen in Maine and the king crab fishermen in Alaska's Bering Strait. Yes, they're all fishermen, which makes them share more of a common bond than they have with roller derby queens, but that bond does not help you.

You should be after fishermen that own bass boats and want to enter competitions. The more narrowly you focus, the fewer people you'll attract but the more strongly you'll attract them.

Question: "But what's wrong with attracting all fishermen and then narrowing it down later?"

Answer: That's better than attracting the *free beer* crowd but is still a waste of time and money. In the amazingly crowded and distracting advertising world we live in, you don't have many shots at getting your message across to any one person. You also have limited resources. If you were a gold miner I suppose you could dig up the entire state of California and eventually find gold. After all, you did narrow your search to California and not the other 49 states. But why wouldn't you make your job easier by first finding a promising vein of ore? That's what highly targeted traffic is, and that's what should be your objective.

MYTH NUMBER THREE: "I'M WAITING FOR THE GAME CHANGER"

I already talked about this in an earlier chapter but it's so prevalent that I cannot overemphasize it.

Many marketers will scratch and claw to stand on top of everyone else and proclaim that they've found the *Silver Bullet* to marketing. They've found the game changer that makes everything else obsolete. I suggest that you roll your eyes and find a better use of your time.

The real game changers are not gimmicks and tricks discovered by a geek in his basement but instead are things we've known about for a while. For instance, the World Wide Web is a game changer because we can finally cut out the middlemen and appeal directly to an audience that will pay us directly. That's phenomenally big news but it's free for the taking—you don't need to buy some guy's system in order to take advantage of it.

The ability to hire specialists from the four corners of the globe to help you with particular projects is a game changer, because no longer do you need to staff an office building to create a thriving business.

Game changers are not things like software programs that claim to exploit some weakness in Google such that you can shoot to the top of the rankings overnight. It may even be true that Google temporarily is unaware of some cute trick that allows a site to pop up in the rankings. If that anomaly is legal then you might even consider using it— just make sure you don't hang your hopes on it working for very long, or you risk the very foundation of your business.

Here's an example of a shady game changer. I know a guy who at one point made a fortune in the online weight-loss supplement business. An average day for him was $10,000 to $20,000 in revenues, most of which was profit. Not bad.

What one of his pals had discovered was a very special blog technique. They posted little images on major news sites—attractive pictures of a woman's bare waist in skin-tight pants, for instance. When you clicked on the image you would be taken to a blog that was called something like

Kathy's Weight-Loss Journal. It would be a pretty pink blog with little flowers in the corner and a lively journal all about Kathy's ongoing challenge with weight loss. It seems that Kathy looked far and wide and could not find anything that worked until a friend told her about the Açaí berry, grown in Brazil and elsewhere.

Practically overnight, Kathy became a new person! She just drank an Açaí berry smoothie in the morning and at lunch but otherwise could eat what she wanted and not even exercise much. The pounds just melted off. Women asked her what was the secret and men asked her out.

Kathy's blog also had a really helpful section where other people could write in. Here's a typical series of messages:

> Joan B: Kathy, is this for real? I mean I've tried everything just like you did and they're all scams!
>
> Kathy: Joan, I know what you mean, girl, but I couldn't believe it! I've even tried other Açaí berry drinks but only this one did the trick for me.
>
> Joan B: Kathy — You're a lifesaver!!!!! I tried your Açaí stuff and I lost 14 pounds in just one week! Ohmygod! Now Josh and I are engaged ☺!

Kathy's blog even has a little corner where you can order her favorite Açaí berry drink. How helpful of her!

The whole thing was a fake. There was no Kathy and no Joan but instead some programmer named Bruno. There was indeed an Açaí berry drink and my friend made a bloody fortune selling it.

That is, until Google caught on to the existence of so many similar blogs and shut down his advertising. He was lucky that only Google caught him because the Federal Trade Commission would not have been as lenient with his false claims.

Other game changers may even be lawful but are just as temporary. Let's remember that Google uses Google too. It knows who's skyrocketing in popularity and it knows a lot about billions of web sites and the connections between them.

Google's business model is designed around two things—profits and providing quality search content for visitors. Anything else is a distraction that potentially harms Google's reputation. If you build your business on gimmicks, don't be surprised when those gimmicks suddenly disappear, along with much of your profits.

MYTH NUMBER FOUR: "IT'S ALL ABOUT COST PER LEAD"

This myth is alive and well. Just the other day I saw a respected marketer trumpet the fact that he's found a super-secret source where his cost per lead was around one penny.

How silly. With our *bikini method* we could get our *cost per lead* to a fraction of a penny. When you go to your local bank branch to make a deposit, it's such a shame that they don't have a line on the deposit slip for *Cost of Lead*. If they did, these marketers would be filthy rich. The last bank deposit slip I saw only had lines for *Cash* and for *Checks*.

That leads me to the first of several crucial principles you need to tattoo onto the inside of your eyelids.

Principle One: The True Measure of a Lead–Generation Technique Is Not *Cost per Lead* but Instead *Return on Investment*

It's the Holy Grail of savvy marketers. If I write a check for $100 and I get a return of $280, or $113, or even just $102, then those may be acceptable results. However obvious that logic may seem to you, it's not a common practice to think that way.

Plenty of marketers are hooked on cheap leads and would never consider paying several dollars per lead, not to mention tens of dollars per lead. I have some lead sources where I'm delighted to pay over $20 per name. Why? Because I measure my ultimate results with those names and I know that statistically those leads will earn me well in excess of $20 each. It's true that I must be patient and cultivate the leads into buyers and eventually into long-term customers. That's okay because I'm in the business for the long term and not for a quick hit.

On the other hand, I've abandoned certain lead sources with a cost-per-lead of under $5 because they did not result in a profitable relationship for me.

One of the best lighthouses you can construct to guide your marketing efforts is to focus on return on investment.

Principle Two: Lead Sources Have a Half–Life Just Like Uranium

Physicists measure the radioactivity of different substances by their *half-life*, or how long it takes for the substance to lose half its radiation strength.

Sources of leads act the same way: Certain new techniques explode on the scene and are gone in a matter of months or even weeks. Others seem to stick around forever. It's fine to have a mixture of the two as long as you realize that they all decay over time to some extent. That means they'll need your periodic attention to reinvigorate them or swap out one technique for another.

Principle Three: There Is No One Single "Best" Lead Source for Everyone

You should build your business on as broad a base of lead sources as you can. One very smart marketer was on a panel discussion at an event and people were astonished at how quickly he could move into a territory and generate business for a new medical practice. Someone asked him, "What one technique do you use to get 80 customers per month when the industry average is only 10 or 20 per month?"

His response: "I don't have one technique that delivers 80 customers to me each month. I have about 80 techniques and each one delivers about one customer per month—and I use all of 'em."

Now that's a broad base on which to build a business. Let's say a few of those techniques have really short half-lives and quickly decay into nothing. This marketer will notice a dip on his lead-source report and can then swap out those techniques for something better—maybe the next new thing. Compare that to the predicament my Açaí berry friend was in, whose single-source business became toast overnight.

Principle Four: Don't Pursue Prospects—Attract Them

In Chapter 1, I (Dave) told you about the millions of dollars I've made by sending letters to potential sellers of real estate asking if they might be interested in selling their property to me. While other investors beat themselves up with the rejection of having doors slammed in their face as they go from house to house, I wait for a motivated seller to call me.

It's how you will stay in the marketing business for a long time and how you will thrive. Maybe you're twice as tough as the next toughest guy with the thickest skin, but continual rejection—year after year—sooner or later will eat through that skin and you'll get out of the business. Avoid that whole world of pain by sending out your message and waiting for people to raise their hands and say, "Tell me more."

It's a paradox, really—the more you pursue people the less they want what you have. But when you make it known that you have something but you're not pushing it on anyone, suddenly the defense mechanisms come down and people open up to you.

The best way to make it known that you have something of value is the fifth and final principle.

Principle Five: Give Before You Get

I discussed this one in Chapter 3 in the context of special reports and it's true with practically all lead-generation sources.

Remember our discussion about kidney stone remedies and how you don't have to be a doctor in order to be successful at marketing such a report? You're not going to be successful if your marketing is nothing other than, "Buy my home remedies for kidney stones." It still is unlikely to work even if you dress it up with smooth promotional language and throw in modifiers like, "The instant you open my amazing *Home Guide to Kidney Stone Relief*, you'll immediately begin to feel better. In fact, by night time you'll not even remember that you ever had kidney stones!"

Of course, everyone but the most desperate sufferers would instantly think *"Yeah right—another snake-oil salesman,"* and stop reading.

But what if you gave some useful information about how to tell that another kidney stone attack was about to happen? And what if you actually listed several things to try in order to make the attacks shorter and less painful? You would not have divulged any of your home remedies but still you'll have delivered valuable information.

Readers might think, "*Okay, this guy knows the pain I've been through because those were my exact symptoms.*"

When you give valuable information it's more powerful than hype, and when you can avoid the hype then you in effect have stopped shouting at people, and that makes them open up to you.

THE MOVING PARTS OF A LEAD-GENERATION EFFORT

Now that we've busted some lead-generation myths and replaced them with profitable principles, let's see how it all comes together in online lead generation.

Step One: Deliver Valuable Information to a Highly Targeted Audience

We just finished talking about that, so you know what's involved.

Step Two: Direct Them to a Specific Page

In other words, you've just captured a bit of their attention and interest by delivering quality information to them. Now what? You want to strengthen the delicate bond you're creating by pointing them to even more helpful information. You should direct them to click over to your web site in order to get that information.

I estimate that 80 percent of businesses get this step wrong. Not only do they market to a far-too-general audience, such as the fishermen example we discussed, but they then direct visitors to the home page of their business.

That is a highly ineffective way to market. It's as if you were the *Customer Service Desk* at a giant warehouse store and a customer just came to you with a question:

"Excuse me, do you have light bulbs?"
"Yes sir! We stock all kinds!"
"Could you please tell me where they are?"
"Oh, they're right here in the store, believe me. Just look around and you'll find them."

As silly as that sounds, when you direct a person to your home page, that's what you're doing.

> Profit Rule: Before you have the name of a visitor, put blinders on that person and deliver only highly tar- geted and relevant information to that person's inter- ests. After you have visitors' names, show them whatever else you want.

There's only one exception to that rule and it's that you can send people to your home page only if your entire site is highly targeted. If you build a custom site just about Schnau- zer grooming, then perhaps your visitors will feel right at home on the home page. But if you have a site all about dog grooming and you're now focused on a Schnauzer grooming info product, you must take them to a page all about that one topic. Those pages are often referred to as *landing pages*.

Question: "But that's a lot of work!"
Answer: So what's your question?
Question: "Can't I just have a Schnauzer Grooming menu
             item on my home page? They can read, after all.
             Won't that be good enough?"
Answer: No you can't, for two reasons. First, you're as-
             suming that they will find the Schnauzer Groom-
             ing link but you might have two dozen other

breeds listed. Their link might be lower on the page and you're now making them hunt for it. In other words, you're too lazy to send them to the right page but you're hoping they won't be too lazy to hunt for the correct link. Bad assumption.

Second, by taking them to the page with all other dog breeds, you've just blown your aura of specialization. People want specialists. If I have a heart condition, I don't want a general practitioner—I want a heart specialist. If visitors absolutely love their cute little Schnauzers and think they're just the finest dogs on the face of the earth, the last thing they want is to be taken to a dog site with 40 other breeds, all getting more or less equal attention.

Step Three: Reinforce that They're in the Right Place

To recap, visitors read a useful article about Schnauzer grooming in Step One and liked what they saw. They then noticed a link at the bottom of that article saying something to the effect of: "This article is by Mary Jones who's a devoted Schnauzer lover. If you would like more tips on how to care for your own Schnauzer, just visit her site at www .SchnauzerSecrets.com." Here's the point of Step Three—when visitors click on that link, make sure they immediately see something reinforcing that they're in the right place.

There's a measurement tool called *bounce rate*, which means how many people arrive on your web page and never click any button before leaving. It's not uncommon for sites to have a 60 to 80 percent bounce rate, or even higher. That means most of those people land on the page, take a glance, and decide, *"That's not what I expected."* Do not go to all the effort to get people to your web page and then have almost all of them bounce. Instead telegraph the message,

"You've come to the right place! Here indeed is more information about your Schnauzer!"

You can do that with a big bold headline, or a picture of an adorable Schnauzer, or maybe both.

Step Four: Reinforce Their Decision to Visit Your Site by Giving Them Even More Information

Most sites manage to get a few visitors only to blow it with an overt *Buy Me! Buy Me!* message. Don't push yourself on them, but instead strengthen that bond by indeed giving them more information about Schnauzer care. Maybe it's the very same grooming topic as you had in the Step One article, but here you go into a bit more detail. You might have more case histories on the site, or a couple of pointers from people who approached a grooming issue in their own unique way. Remember that the targeted readers of this page are passionate about Schnauzers, so you really can't overdo it.

Step Five: Explain There's Even More Where that Came From

This is where you make your offer. You have attracted their attention and given them valuable information. You've had them take action by clicking to your web page and they realized it is in fact about their precious Schnauzers. You have practiced the principle of *Give Before You Get* by giving this helpful information.

Even with all that choreography it's not yet time to sell them a product! You're at the beginning of the first conversation, okay? It's a little premature to talk about marriage.

It's instead time to sell them on giving you their contact information. You say something like:

I've just completed a new report on 16 more grooming secrets just for Schnauzers. As we know, they're not like other breeds. I'd be happy to send that report to your e-mail inbox if you put your contact information in the box below. If you like, you can click the link below and see my privacy policy but here it is in short: I will never sell or rent your name. I respect the privacy of other Schnauzer owners and would never violate that. I'll just use that contact information to send you the report and other Schnauzer information from time to time. You can unsubscribe from my private list any time you want and you'll never hear from me again.

All the privacy language is important. People are so sick and tired of spam that you must gain their trust in order for them to give you their name. I don't blame them because I feel the same way.

Warning: Do Not Just Have an E-Mail Box for Them to Fill Out and Then Take Them Directly to the Report.

If you do that, you'll just have captured a huge number of garbage names along with a few legitimate ones. Why? Because most people are tired of the tricks and the spam so they play a trick of their own. When asked for their e-mail address they write down nonsense like foofoofoo@foofoo .com just so they can get past the current screen and grab the special report.

Therefore, at the very least this is what you must say: "I'd be happy to send that report to your e-mail inbox if you put your contact information in the box below. . . ." They then get the message that if they want that special report, they must give you a valid e-mail address because that's where you will send the report.

I have made millions of dollars by going further than that. Most of the time I request their full name, e-mail, and street address, and they give it to me because I tell them that I will *mail a hardcopy of the report to them*. Why do I bother to do that? Because I appreciate how valuable a good lead is and I'd like to be able to contact them in multiple ways. Most of my communications are via e-mail, but occasionally I send postcards, letters, or short newsletters to my prospects. By mixing up the media I employ to reach them, I have a better chance of having them actually receive and read my message. I know that I'm in a tiny minority of marketers who capture full contact information but I also know how highly profitable it's been to me.

By the way, even if I occasionally don't ask for a street address, I always ask at least for first name and e-mail. When I then send an e-mail in the future, I can personalize it with their first name.

Step Six: When They Submit Their Contact Information, Instantly Have It Go into Your Database and Redirect Them to a Welcome Page

Many marketers are lazy. Frequently, after visitors leave their name and hit the *Send* button in order to get a report, they're left wondering if the message even went through.

In a later chapter I talk about the e-mail *autoresponder* mechanism you'll use to communicate with prospects, but suffice it to say that your web form will instantly log their contact details and you should redirect them to a page that says:

"Thanks for requesting my report on Schnauzer Grooming Secrets. You can check your inbox for that information. In the meantime, if you have any questions or comments you can reach me by filling in the form below. I look forward to sharing my grooming secrets with you and maybe talking with you soon! Regards, [Your Name]."

Notice how I referred to the specific report in the thank-you message. I also opened the door to hear from them. Who knows—you may have a highly motivated person who's already willing to buy whatever you have. That should not come as a surprise to you because during this entire process you have distinguished yourself from the competition by being not pushy but helpful.

GREAT SOURCES FOR LEADS

The six steps we just covered for capturing a lead are pretty much the same steps no matter where you'll advertise, with minor exceptions. Now let's look at each of the lead sources that I've found to be the most productive.

Pay-Per-Click Advertising

This is one of my most favorite methods of generating quality leads. Pay-per-click advertising is also known as *PPC*. The way it works is you pay a search engine like Google to give you visibility. First, let's make sure you know what PPC advertising looks like on a search engine page. Take a look at Figure 5.1.

When a visitor types a term into Google, the page Google delivers can be divided into three zones.

The *Top Zone* and *Right Zone* contain ads that advertisers pay for. The *Left Zone* is the traditional area that contains results based on Google's estimate of how valuable those web pages are to visitors. In other words, the top and right zones are immediately available to you as a web site owner, provided that you pay for that access. The left zone is known as the *organic rankings*, and it's free but only available to you if you impress Google through a process we'll discuss later.

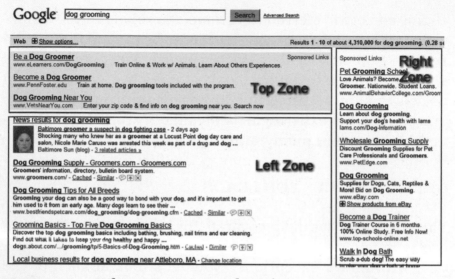

FIGURE 5.1   Where You Can Advertise on a Google Web Page

Several search engines offer PPC advertising but we'll use Google as an example because they're by far the biggest player. Google's PPC service is called *AdWords*. The way PPC works is web sites bid for visibility. Google constantly tweaks its system and what you see on the screen varies between topics people search for, but in general the top zone contains the first two or three PPC listings. They're called *ranks*.

Typically the first to third ranks are in the top zone, and then ranks four, five, and so forth are the ads you see running down the page in the right zone. Depending on the competitiveness of the search term, you can have page after page of PPC ads running down that right zone. In other words, for an extremely competitive term like *life insurance*, you might be ranked #152.

What you will pay is totally determined by an auction market for each search term. Let's take a relatively standard example. Say you wanted to be found for *dog grooming*.

Using a special interface, you would tell Google that you would like to be found for that term, also known as a *key phrase*. Perhaps there's a very hot market for that term and 25 other marketers want to be found for it—that's not unrealistic for a term like *dog grooming*.

As I said before, Google cares about two things in life—making money and delivering a good search experience to visitors. Therefore, the company that's willing to pay Google the most will appear in the number one spot for dog grooming. However, you can earn brownie points for having quality ads and quality web pages. That means, if two advertisers bid the same amount, the higher-quality advertiser will win over the lower-quality advertiser.

You don't pay Google if people simply see your ad, but you only pay if people click on that ad and Google delivers them to your web page.

Bids for key phrases range from about 10 cents to—hang onto your hat—$50. That's correct: For certain absurdly competitive terms like *Scottsdale DUI attorney*, the going rate when someone merely clicks on an ad to find a drunk-driving attorney is 50 bucks.

Hey, that's what the market will bear. Remember our return on investment discussion earlier? These attorneys know the amount of money they'll make in order to represent a person charged with drunk driving and they can do the math: *"Let's see, I'm willing to spend a total of $900 to get a client who will pay me $4,000 to represent him. That means I can afford to have 18 people click on that ad at $50 per click, in the hope that one of them will become my client."* If another Scottsdale attorney can charge higher fees or is willing to work on a smaller profit margin then he might outbid Mr. Fifty Bucks and be willing to spend $55.

Here's the interesting flipside: Don't be elated if your clicks only cost you a dime apiece—if those clicks don't result in a sale. That may seem obvious but I'm continually amazed at how marketers will be delirious with pleasure at cheap lead sources but not calculate what really counts—*How much did I spend and how much did I get back?*

Back to how AdWords works: Your bid and the quality of your ad and web page all determine the rank of that ad. It's fairly useless for your ad to be shown on page 2, 3, or 30 of the results. Think back to how you personally use Google. When you search for something do you scour page after page of results? I'm guessing not, because you'll either see something interesting on page one or you adjust the search term and see what fresh results you get. Only the most highly motivated customers will search page after page.

Question: "But aren't highly motivated customers the very ones we want?"

Answer: Good question! Yes, we want them but the problem is there are so few of them. The other problem is, by hanging out on page 5 or 10, we're keeping our fingers crossed that they get to us. I'd rather have a highly targeted ad on page one and get to my motivated buyers faster and more reliably.

Therefore, you should pay what you need to pay in order to be in the top seven or eight ad spots, so they are visible to visitors without their having to scroll down.

Question: "Don't I want to be in the number one spot? Why should I settle for less?"

Answer: The problem with the number one rank is you're likely to pay much more money than the number two rank. That's because a lot of ego drives that first position:

"Look Boss, I got us to Number One in Google!"

"Well done, Perkins, would you like a raise?"

The other problem is many people who click on the top ad are unmotivated browsing people and not buyers. They're the same guys who are click-happy during television commercials and must scan through a dozen stations at every opportunity. They're not your buyers, but when you sit in the top rank, you'll pay each time they click.

You're likely to get almost as much visibility but at a considerably lower cost by being in ranks two through six or so.

What you say in your ads is extremely important. You have only a handful of words to get across your message, so literally every word and punctuation mark counts.

Entire books cover the topic of Google AdWords and we can't cover all the principles here, but keep this in mind: You're not trying to sell them on anything in your ad. All you need to do is arouse their curiosity. Their eyes will breeze over many ads in a fraction of a second and your ad must stand out by being interesting. Here are three of the best ways to do that.

One: Ask a question. People tend to stop and think when you ask a short, pithy question. It's a superb way to create involvement.

Schnauzer Hair Snafu?
How I Solved My Dog's Grooming
Nightmare, Once and for All.
SchnauzerGroomingSecrets.com

Two: Feel their pain. A short, bold statement can make them feel like, *"Hey, you're one of us."*

They Just Won't Ever Know
What Kidney Stone Pain Is Like

Proven Home Remedies
KidneyStoneReliefSecrets.com

Three: Give before you get. When you mention a free report on a compelling topic you will stand out from most other ads.

Organic Heirloom Tomatoes
It Doesn't Get Any Better, Right?
Free Report With 13 Great Tips
OrganicTomatoSecrets.com

When people click on your ad, they'll be taken to a page that you specify to Google. Remember the key concept we talked about before—you simply must deliver them to a page that reinforces just the thing they're searching for.

That means not dumping them onto your home page, unless the site is totally devoted to organic heirloom gardening tips. If it's instead all about organic gardening, for maximum effectiveness be sure to take them to the heirloom-tomato page.

If you think your customers are different and they have a much-longer attention span and patience than other customers, you're making a tragic mistake. Here's a principle that will serve you well.

Profit Principle: Design your ads and web pages to work for the most impatient and distracted person you know. Don't make that person hunt! If that person can quickly grasp your message, then so will the rest of your readers.

There's another excellent reason to deliver relevant content on your landing page relating to the search term people typed in: Google measures how long readers stay on your page, also known as *engagement*. If Google detects that many people land on your page and immediately click to leave, they will whack your *quality score* for that key phrase. That means you will pay more to rank in a given position versus an advertiser with a better quality score.

Key Phrase Techniques

Remember that the entire AdWords process begins when you tell Google the key phrases you want to be found for—in other words, when a visitor types in those terms, you want your ad to show up.

It's worth becoming proficient at choosing these phrases. In our earlier example, I mentioned the key phrase *dog grooming* and how there's most likely a lot of competition around that phrase. It's almost certainly too broad of a term for you to use because you need to put yourself in visitors' shoes when they type in that term.

Are they searching for dog grooming supplies? Dog grooming tips? Dog grooming centers? Dog grooming for short-hair Chihuahuas—or maybe for long-haired Afghan hounds? Yet if you want your ad to show for the broad term *dog grooming*, Google will be only too happy to take your money and follow your instructions.

You're much better off by becoming highly specific to your information product, which in turn should be specific. Therefore, you might have terms like: Schnauzer grooming, how to groom a Schnauzer, Schnauzer care, Schnauzer fur, Schnauzer hair, and so on.

This is where your research on the topic will come in handy because you should have discovered the *insider language* of the hobby. For instance, lovers of Yorkshire Terriers often call them *Yorkies*. So the key phrase list should contain not only terms like *Yorkshire Terrier grooming*, but also *Yorkie grooming*. Your ad might even be more effective with the slang than with the *outsider's* term of *Yorkshire Terrier*.

Google has an outstanding tool for you to use to research key phrases. Its location changes from time to time so just go to Google and type in *Google keyword tool*. You'll be taken to a free and exceedingly powerful tool.

Just type in a general phrase and Google will quickly show you all the related phrases people use. You can then click a few buttons and add those phrases to your list. Google will even estimate for you the number of visitors that search for the term and the rough amount of competition for the term.

By the way, the Google keyword tool is an excellent place for you to do some info product research, too. You may put in the term *dog grooming* and discover there is a very active search community around some narrow topic like *non-electric grooming techniques* or whatever, and it might be a topic you'd never have thought of on your own.

Also, remember to use misspellings, which can be an overlooked goldmine. If I had an info product having to do with *crème de menthe*, I would be well-advised to list other key phrases like *cream de menthe, cream de mint, crème de mint, crème di ment,* and probably a dozen other variations. All those visitors are after the same concept but spell it every which way. Your competition may think, *"Well anybody who knows the slightest thing about crème de menthe will spell it correctly"*—and that would be a mistaken assumption.

Terms related to your competition are another fruitful resource. If Joe Blow is a powerful force in the Schnauzer grooming community, then you might ask Google to show your ad whenever someone types in *Joe Blow Schnauzers*. Of course, I'm not suggesting that you say anything nasty about him, but simply have Google show your ad when someone types in his name.

Occasionally, you'll get a letter from a well-known person asking you not to use his or her name in any way. For instance, Oprah Winfrey is famous for having an army of lawyers watching for any use of her name whatsoever. If you ever use such names and get a letter, it's an easy matter to tell Google to delete that key phrase from your list.

Google AdSense

You may have heard the term *AdSense* and wonder how that's different from *AdWords*. When you use AdWords, you're paying Google to stick your little ad on its web site for visitors to see. When you use AdSense, you rent space on your site and allow Google to stick other people's ads on your site, and Google pays you for that privilege. How great is that?

Warning: Do Not Use AdSense on Your Landing Pages!

The answer is it's not great to use AdSense on your landing pages. Your grandmother would have called it *penny wise and pound foolish*.

Think what you're doing when you use AdSense on your landing page. You've labored to create a good info product and have further labored to drive visitors to your web site. You recognize that they're highly distractible people whose attention you have for mere seconds before they decide to bail out of your web site and go check the sports scores. You have carefully fanned the spark of their attention so it turned into a small flame, which just might result in their signing up for your special report and then—you allow Google to direct them to someone else's site and most likely not return? How stupid is that?

Using our romance analogy, it's as if you went to all the effort to get the attention of that special someone, say the right words, cultivate the relationship, build a bond, and right when you have the chance for something serious, you stick in an Elvis impersonator in your place because he slipped you a couple bucks.

This gets back to the rule I gave you earlier: Before you have the contact information of your visitors, do not distract them with anything. Only deliver good, solid, believable content and offer to deliver even more content if the visitors leave their contact information. Only then can you afford the luxury of distraction. Once you have their contact information, you can redirect them to your home page with all sorts of interesting diversions on it.

I can assure you that your marketing competition does not get this concept but instead drools at the possibility of making a few dollars from AdSense. Google is smart for tempting them but you're also smart for not falling for the temptation. You will instead cultivate those visitors into a significant income stream, not one-time pennies from AdSense.

I've covered Google AdWords here, but once you have that up and running, you'll be able to set up more or less the same types of advertising campaigns on other PPC services like Microsoft's *Bing* and Yahoo!'s *Sponsored Search*. They have different labels for things but pretty much work the same way.

What you may find over time is that the most passionate dog lovers are found through one of those services and the most passionate tomato growers seem to be at another service. I don't know why that is, but I do know that it's worth testing the various PPC services to see how they differ for a given product. Remember to test different PPC services for each info product you launch because results could vary from one product to the next.

Organic Search

Earlier I mentioned the term *organic rankings* to describe that *left zone* of results on a Google page. I also may have tantalized you with the statement that those listings are free.

They are indeed free but you must earn the right to appear in that left zone through the quality of your web pages and their popularity. An entire industry has sprung up to help you get your pages ranked organically—the business is called *search engine optimization*, or *SEO* for short.

About the only thing as secret as the formula for Coca-Cola is the formula for how Google ranks web sites for organic search. Google has said that it takes several hundred factors into account when arriving at its rankings. Even though we don't have the exact formula, we do know from Google that several large and fundamental factors determine the visibility of a web page. Let's look at them.

Major Factor: Who Links to Your Site
Google was started by two Stanford students who had a revelation. They concluded that there was no way they could review and rate the quality and value of each web page on the Internet. They then realized that they didn't have to rate the quality but instead could notice which pages received the most links and traffic from other pages.

After all, if someone builds a great site devoted to kite flying, pretty soon the kite community will be buzzing about that new site. People will link to that site from other sites, blogs, e-mails, and all over the web. The Google guys realized that they could quite effectively predict the quality and value of sites by monitoring who was linking to whom.

Major Factor: What Is the Theme of Your Page

Google does not employ dozens of PhD wizards in linguistics, physics, statistics, and other fields for their fashion sense but instead to make Google's software smarter by the day. One of its challenges is to send a *spider* or *robot*—it's nothing more than a small computer program—to most pages on the web on a regular basis. Google calls it the *Googlebot*. When the Googlebot visits your web page it tries to make sense of what it sees. It cannot understand pictures on the site but instead looks at other factors, one of which is the nature of the words on the page.

Googlebot scans your Schnauzer page and notices that there seem to be many references to Schnauzers, grooming, pet hair, and so forth. The Googlebot also looks at the pages linking to your Schnauzer page and notices that they say things like, "For a great article about how to groom your Schnauzer to win the dog show, just go to www.Schnauzer GroomingSecrets.com."

Googlebot concludes that not only does your web page talk a lot about Schnauzers, but even other sites refer to you in Schnauzer terms. If those other sites had links that said, "*Here's a good dog site*," then Googlebot might not conclude you were all about Schnauzers.

It's in this way that Google arrives at its own conclusions about what your page is about. Wouldn't it be valuable to have Google actually tell you what it thinks is the theme of your page? Well, you can. Just go to the Google Keyword

Tool I spoke about earlier and look for a button called *Website Content*. When you click it you should be able to enter a web address and Google will return a long list of words it thinks are what that page is about.

You may very well be shocked at what Google thinks is the page topic versus what you had intended. This is good news because now you can adjust the content of the page so that over time Google does in fact think it's about *organic heirloom tomatoes*, and not about *compost bins* or whatever.

Do you see why general pages with all sorts of stuff on them are great for lazy marketers but bad for getting found? Google looks to deliver highly targeted answers to very specific questions people type in. When you create detailed, useful, relevant pages that are tied to one narrow concept, you'll shoot to the top of the rankings, above all the general pages that kinda sorta are about a given topic.

Getting Found Locally in Google

Google recently came out with an excellent tool for anyone who wishes to market to a geographic location. On the one hand, if you're offering that kidney stone remedy info product you really don't care where your customers come from.

However, what if you are a plastic surgeon, plumber, home builder, or real estate agent and you mostly get business from a 20- to 50-mile radius from your office? For that matter, what if you have any info product that might appeal to a local market like offering a list of *Chicago attractions* for tourists?

When you type that sort of local term into Google, a special type of map usually appears, like the one in Figure 5.2.

FIGURE 5.2 Google Has a Different System for When You Want to Get Found in Your Local Market

These maps are powerful marketing tools because people's eyes are immediately drawn to the map and who is listed first. The map appears at or near the top of the first page of Google results for that term so it gets great visibility.

How you get on that map is a whole separate skill from how you appear on the rest of Google's results. Notice the little marker with the letter "A" on it and how the Shedd Aquarium has 211 reviews. That gives you a clue that getting reviews of your product or service is very important to Google. Keep in mind that visitors of the human variety are also highly influenced by lots of solid, positive reviews.

On the other hand, notice how the company in fifth position—letter "E"—has only 39 reviews but is above the company in letter "F" with 137 reviews. Therefore, the fact that you have lots of reviews is not the only factor Google considers.

One way to boost your ranking in this sort of page is to type in *Google Places* and register with Google. The more they know about who you are, where you're located, and what people think of you, the better. If you don't take this little-known step, Google may not know you even exist and you could easily be left off the map entirely.

There are many more factors involved in getting a top geographical ranking in Google. If you would like more information, go to www.sixfiguresecondincome.com and type the term "Local Search" into the search box and I'll send you a more detailed report.

Article Marketing

Google loves good-quality articles and so do humans. Think about your own way of searching for information on the Web. If you type in a search phrase and are taken to an article with answers to your specific question, think of all the good things that happen:

- You like Google because it quickly delivered a good search result to you.
- Google likes the article writer because it was solid, helpful information.
- The article writer has credibility because he or she delivered useful content without screaming: *Buy Me! Buy Me!*

Throughout all the fads in the Internet marketing world, article marketing has continued to be a highly potent way to become visible, and new web sites can benefit from articles just as well as established sites can.

The reality is that most marketers are too lazy to write a decent, short article. Instead they squirm in their seats and look for any way to avoid writing solid content.

For instance, they decide they'd rather use Twitter and leave messages like, *I'm eating a ham on rye right now.* That isn't going to do anything for your reputation within Google, let me tell you.

Marketers sometimes resort to robot article writers, which promise to turn out thousands of articles while you sleep. They operate on a simple principle: You tell me the key phrase you want to be found for, and my machine will pump out an article for you in a nanosecond.

These were all the rage for a few years because they held the promise of making a fortune for the laziest, most slothful marketer. Unfortunately, the type of article they produced read something like this:

> "Want to know about Schnauzer grooming? You've come to the right place about Schnauzer grooming because when it comes to grooming Schnauzers, we've been at it a long time. See, Schnauzer grooming is different from other dog grooming because . . ."

A machine could turn out this garbage because all it had to do was use a template and replace "Schnauzer grooming" with "kite flying" and the article would then be all about kite flying.

The only people who made money with these scams were the marketers peddling the article robots to unsuspecting newbie marketers. Google quickly caught on to this nonsense and stopped recognizing such articles, whereupon the scam artists moved overseas. They dumped the robots for humans—in other words, poor people in third-world countries. They often spoke broken English but would create human-written articles for pennies.

These services may have fared a little better in Google but any American reading the article would be left thinking, *"Huh? What was that? This article isn't helpful at all."*

That brings us back to writing simple articles with an emphasis on *simple*. Here's all you have to do:

- Know your specific topic and have two or three genuinely helpful pointers or examples.
- Write an article of between 250 and 450 words. That's really very little.
- Create a compelling title that arouses curiosity and is highly relevant to a search term you want to be known for.
- Incorporate that search term a few times in the article without overdoing it.
- Have a *resource box* at the bottom that says a few words about you and directs readers to your specific, targeted web page for more detailed information.

One guy I know is a Captain on active duty in the U.S. Army. He works long hours but comes home, relaxes a while, and then knocks out an article or two each night on targeted topics. Within a short time his article revenues exceeded his military pay and he'll soon retire from the Army with a six-figure income purely from his article writing.

He didn't attend any fancy college or discover any whiz-bang super-secret gimmick for scamming the search engines into giving him high rankings. No, he just put one foot in front of the other and cranked out tiny articles on a regular basis.

If you would like to find out my current recommended resources for using articles to get found in the search engines, go to www.sixfiguresecondincome.com and type "articles" into the search box.

Social Media

By now you know my opinion that a great deal of social media is hype. As Seth Godin so accurately phrased it, many of these sites like Facebook and Twitter are fabulous ways to burn up hours per day being unproductive.

Nevertheless, I would not dismiss them without giving them a try for your business. Of course, I cannot know what sort of info product you have in mind. Certain age groups seem to have some of these social media sites surgically implanted in their brains, so reaching them via a Facebook video or other posting might be highly effective.

When you use these services, be sure to keep your *ROI meter* on at all times. Even though services like Twitter are free, the question becomes: *What kind of return are you getting for your investment of time?* If you can deputize your niece or nephew with the brain implant to become your surrogate on these services, you might have stumbled onto a moneymaker. Just don't be romanced into doing this or any other single marketing technique simply because someone gives you a line about *"Everyone's doing it,"* or *"I have 85,000 followers."* Nod your head and then say, "That's nice. If you're trying to impress me then show me the money you can *prove* came from this tool."

Blogs

These are a hybrid between social media and articles. A few years ago blogs were touted as the new phenomenon that would revolutionize the Internet and render all other techniques obsolete. It was kind of like teenagers concluding that older generations were idiots and world peace was coming as soon as they got a chance to run things.

Well, even though they haven't revolutionized the earth, blogs have matured into valuable tools. You can't watch the evening news without seeing a political analyst who writes for a blog. They also have the benefit of incorporating a technology called an *RSS feed*, which allows the blogs to bypass e-mail spam filters and be delivered right to the subscribers' news-reader tools. That can be very handy in our spam-saturated world.

A number of blogs also have achieved recognition by Google as being influential sites. Simply type any current event into Google and you're likely to see some of the top results being occupied by blogs. You can usually identify that a site is a blog because it has the long *comments* section at the bottom of every article or entry, though the line is blurring between blogs and other types of sites.

One really excellent way to bring attention to your info product is to search for blogs in your field of interest. Go to Google and type in *directory of blogs* and then search for your topic at one of the big blog sites. Also, just search for the topic directly in Google. Now look at the articles and entries you see and determine how you can add value.

Notice that I said *determine how you can add value* and I did not say *tell them what you have for sale.* You need to give before you get and you must make it clear from your helpful comments that you know something about the topic. Then at the bottom of the comments where your name appears you can usually mention your web site. No overt promotion is necessary, but just a simple mention. That way you won't annoy casual readers but still can be contacted by people who think, *"Hey that was good stuff—I wonder if she has any more?"*

YouTube

Google bought YouTube years ago because Google could see the direction the Web was taking toward exponentially more video. Smart investment.

Is it the *be-all-end-all* for your marketing efforts? Probably not, but as with everything else we've discussed it's worth uploading some relevant videos to YouTube to see what kind of results you get.

Instead of creating a special report for your info product you could do a demonstration, short presentation, interview, or anything else that might grab the attention of your audience.

One of my favorite examples is the *Will it blend?* series of videos by a company called BlendTec. They make food blenders. On the one hand, who could blame them if the company thought, *"But our situation's different—we make blenders! We're not a rock band or a cool new flying car. Who's going to watch us make a smoothie?"*

They could have thought that but they didn't. Some genius decided to blend golf balls in front of the video camera and the blender reduced them to powder. Then they made another video where they blended a broomstick, and later a digital camera, garden hose, marbles, and finally a brand-new, just-introduced, hard-to-find iPhone.

The videos were an online sensation, getting more than 83 million viewers! When they ground up the iPhone, they sold the powder on eBay for $901. And if you think all this was just a silly publicity stunt, revenues at BlendTec have gone up more than 700 percent. That really is the genius of thinking *outside the box*.

If you can come up with a great demonstration of something then more power to you—but don't even try to hit a home run at first. Just talk about your product as if you were telling another Schnauzer enthusiast about some of the techniques you've found to be most helpful. Let the quality of your message do the selling for you.

You don't need fancy equipment to record video for YouTube. Go to Amazon.com and search for highly rated video recorders. One bit of advice: You really should try to get a camera with an external microphone jack. Otherwise, you'll sound like you're recording in an empty tank and it will distract from your message.

Press Releases

This is yet another example of the Internet revolutionizing a previously painful process. How painful?

In the Bad Old Days you had to spend hundreds of dollars to hire a publicist, or you could spend less money but way more time learning the craft of writing press releases. Then you had to study the publications you wanted your press release to appear in. You wrote your press release, faxed it to the editor, put your hands together, and prayed.

Then you waited. If you called the editor you ran the risk of appearing pushy or at least a pest. Maybe you got lucky and your press release got published. In that case, it most likely gave you 24 hours of visibility until the following day's paper got published, or you got perhaps a month of traction if your story got into a magazine.

The Internet shattered that model. Now you can go online and for somewhere between free and $200 you can send out your release. The online services have helpful guides to writing effective press releases and it's also easy to see lots of current examples right there on the site. For a few dollars more you can have a professional editor review and tweak your press release.

In the old model, editors had to pick and choose their press releases for only the most newsworthy items because they had only so much space to work with. The Internet has no space limitations, so as long as your press release meets certain basic requirements for good English and a clear message, it will be posted quickly—typically the next day.

More good news: It's possible for your press release to be picked up by Google and other major search engines in a matter of hours. That's because Google is voracious for fresh information so it has a pipeline right to the press release services. I've had press releases issued at midnight and by 5:00 AM Google, Yahoo!, and other major players already had my information built into their search results.

In this new world your information can stick around longer, too. Because there is no space constraint, Google and the other services will continue to *index* or show your information for months or even years.

Before you get too excited let me give you a couple of pointers. First, your press release must have a clear, crisp theme. Remember our discussion about how Google determines the theme of web pages and ranks them accordingly? The same is true with press releases. If you issue one about dog grooming it will be so vague that Google will bury it under a heap of other items related to dog grooming.

Your best approach is to use that crisp key phrase like *Schnauzer grooming advice*—or whatever your keyword search told you was popular and searched for. In just the same way that you constructed a page or an article around the key phrase, you now construct a press release. You can literally be found for that term overnight.

If you would like my current recommendations for press release services then go to www.sixfiguresecondincome .com and type "press release" into the search box.

eBay

I suspect if you asked your friends, "What is eBay?" you would hear, "It's an auction site." Though that's true, eBay is in reality a search engine for people who have their credit cards in their hands and are ready to buy.

For instance, a great deal of eBay transactions occur not through auction, but at a fixed price. eBay also allows the sale of info products. Because eBay is such a vast market-place, you'll find plenty of garbage products along with the good ones, but that should not concern you. Instead you should focus on having eBay list your product for the specific terms you want to be known for. They make that easy—you simply tell eBay what you want to be listed under and pay a few extra pennies for that service.

There's another entire hidden use for eBay that few people take advantage of—the classified section. You can pay around $10 and have a whole ebay page up for 30 days. The best part is you're allowed to include a phone number and also capture names of people who are interested in your materials. That's powerful because you can capture not only buyers' names, but just tire-kickers or leads. For around 10 bucks eBay will give you visibility for a month—that's a great deal.

Here's another powerful technique that few people have a clue about. If you create a *Featured Listing* in eBay's auction system, Google will pick up that listing right in the Google main results—the left zone we talked about earlier. This is good stuff. Remember how I said that section is reserved for people who earn those organic listings through their reputation and page quality? Well, in this case, you get to piggyback on eBay's monster reputation so, when you pay eBay around $20, you get high visibility under both ebay and Google for that specific term.

Again, don't expect to rank highly for a really general term because the competition is not only fierce, but you'll only get wishy-washy leads partially interested in your product. Go for highly specific terms and you can own them, one by one.

Question: "What good is my *Featured Listing* visibility on Google after that particular auction expires on eBay?"

Answer: If you take full advantage of your auction listing, you'll fill out the *About Me* section in the upper-right corner. That allows you to show people a small video that, when clicked, can take them to your web site. It's beyond the scope of this book to list the programming necessary, but it's an inexpensive task to get a programmer to do it for you once, and you can then use it over and over.

Inexpensive and Great Offline Strategies for Getting Found

I'm a big fan of all the excellent online strategies we've just covered, but I don't want to fall into the trap I told you about before—the trap of saying that the traditional stuff is dead and only the new techniques work.

It's for that reason that you should consider a number of offline techniques to generate leads. We already discussed how e-book reports can be fine but sometimes you're better off with printed reports that hang around and get read more. It can be the same with other offline techniques in the sense that they're tangible.

Local Newspapers

These can be solid sources of leads because they're always looking for content. You won't be paid anything when you contribute a story and you might not realize much fame other than the most local variety. Still, you're likely to find a willing editor and audience for your message.

One added bonus: Many local newspapers have online versions where your story can live long after it runs in the daily paper. Be sure to mention your target key phrases in the article or interview. That way, when the piece is in the online version of the newspaper, there's a good chance it will get picked up by Google, which, as you now know, likes anything news-related.

Question: "If local papers are good, wouldn't big-city papers be better?"

Answer: You can get plenty of exposure in big-city papers, but they'll charge you an arm and a leg for it. They give great deals to huge car dealerships that run ads every day, but they really nail the little guy in the price department. I wouldn't bother.

Free–Standing Inserts

When you get to the point where you have a few hundred dollars this is a splendid way to get your message across in local papers. You've no doubt been the recipient of free-standing inserts, or FSIs. They are single sheets of note-book-size paper inserted into the middle of newspapers. Because it seems that nobody's caught on to this marketing channel, the price is really low. You can have the newspaper print both sides of a full sheet of notebook paper and they'll deliver it inside the newspaper for typically less than the cost of a two-inch-high ad in the paper. The difference is you have far more visibility.

Commuter Newspapers

If you live in a larger metropolitan area, you've seen these newspapers specifically targeted at commuters. What a great captive audience! They're tired of working and are on a train or bus with not much to do. They'll spend more time looking at your ad than if they were home.

These papers are often free for readers and reasonably priced for advertisers. The downside is you have a very general audience so your offer might work best if it's applicable to the road-warrior, cubicle-dweller type of reader. One source for many of these publications is www.echo-media.com.

Local Clubs and Events

If you use the meetup.com service I mentioned earlier, you may find local clubs or events relevant to your product. These outfits often have mailers, bulletin boards, and online or printed newsletters. Try these methods of getting the word out on your product, especially the news that you have a free special report. Then you can gather members' contact information and market to them over time.

Direct Mail

People call direct mail *junk mail*, but it's only junk if the message is general and hyped. Direct mail can be a fabulous lead generator when it's a simple postcard to a targeted audience with an offer of a free special report. Many national groups or associations—or even those local clubs—are eager to rent their mailing lists at pennies per name for relevant offers.

Warning: Direct Mail DOES Work. Don't Listen to Naysayers Who Wrote Lousy Ads and Now Blame Direct Mail for the Lack of Response.

No doubt Uncle Moe once tried direct mail and it didn't work. The truth is that he probably tried a lousy offer of *Buy me! Buy me!* once, and of course that didn't work.

With direct mail and most other advertising methods you need patience to give before you get, and then try different offers. Once you have an ad and offer that works in the Google AdWords world, you'll have some good market intelligence to try over in the direct-mail world.

Question: "What's a good response rate if I do a mailing?"
Answer: Elsewhere you'll read plenty of conflicting answers to that question. Some people will say a 2 to 3 percent response rate to a mailing is solid, and you should get at least 1 percent.

That's baloney. The only true answer is our old friend, *return on investment*. If I have a tenth-of-one-percent response rate but my advertising costs are low and my profit margin is high, I could have an excellent ROI. On the other hand, people will brag about their 5 or 10 percent response rate without realizing—or admitting—that their costs were so high compared to their revenues that they actually lost money on that effort.

ROI is the financial compass that will keep you pointed toward profits and away from trouble.

* * *

We've come a long way so far—we've covered lots of myths and built a solid foundation of principles for your info business. We've created a product, cultivated an online presence, and attracted leads. Now it's time to say and do the right things that will persuade those leads to pay you and thus become customers.

CHAPTER 6

How to Turn Prospects into Buyers

Have you noticed how sometimes the most profound things are the simplest to state? When it comes to getting people to buy your info product—or any other product or service under the sun—there's a plain, profound truth: Your task is nothing more than attention and persuasion.

That's it. You cannot hope to persuade them before you have their attention, but attention is not enough. They may hang on your every word, but if you do not then persuade them to buy, it's all been for nothing.

Fortunately for us, most businesspeople have no clue how to get attention constructively and persuade profitably. They blunder around and make our job easier because it's not hard to outdo them.

As we did at the beginning of this book, let's look at the major mistakes marketers make. We'll then go through a clear, step-by-step process for selling just about anything under the sun.

 MISTAKE NUMBER ONE: INEFFECTIVE MARKETERS CONFUSE ATTENTION WITH SHOUTING

Shouting has its place in our lives. For instance, if you're at a sports stadium or rock concert the only way you might be able to communicate is through shouting. Yelling at people is also completely appropriate when they're about to step off a curb into the path of an oncoming vehicle. In that case, the shout telegraphs the message, *"Freeze because your life depends on it!"*

You're most likely the victim of marketers misusing shouting. They seem to think, *"Hey, if I can get people to stop dead in their tracks and pay attention, they'll buy more of my stuff."* No, they won't. They'll just turn off to your hyped message.

One example of this nonsense is a famous ad that went like this:

SEX!!!
Now that I have your attention,
I'd like to talk about life insurance. . . .

Yes, many of us are hard-wired to pay attention to the "s" word, but this is a cheap shot.

Other marketers are notorious for sending letters in those brown government-looking envelopes with *Official Tax-Related Business* stamped on the outside. The normal reaction is to tear open the letter, half-expecting an IRS audit notice concerning your tax return. Instead the letter contains some nonsense like: "We at Schmedlap and Perkins Tax Accountants would like to offer you a free consultation about your tax needs. . . ."

A third variation is the type of e-mail you've probably received with a subject line like: "Emergency—Open Up." When you open the e-mail it's just the same-old ho-hum nonsense about whatever product the marketer is flogging. There was no emergency.

I just scratch my head at this stuff. *Whom do they think they're kidding with all the fake urgency?* There is a theory that a small percentage of the population will be suckers for absolutely anything. They're the ones who give their life savings over to scam artists, and who try to buy Viagra at a 95 percent discount through the mail from someone in Singapore. Maybe that hype does work for the tiniest sliver of the population, or else we probably wouldn't be victims of so much spam every day.

This book is not about getting you a tiny sliver of business from zombie consumers who will buy anything. It's about showing you how to sell with integrity and honesty, and how to attract a far larger market that's looking for honest marketers for a change.

 ## MISTAKE NUMBER TWO: INEFFECTIVE MARKETERS BOOST THEIR CLAIMS OUT OF ALL PROPORTION

This is a variation on the theme of shouting to get your attention. In this case, the marketers can only find extreme words to use to describe things.

For instance, if they were let loose on an organic heirloom tomato product, they might say something like:

> And when you get my guide, you'll be absolutely amazed at how you can grow truckloads of tomatoes with ease!! And that's not all! Your neighbors will mistake your tomato patch for red pumpkins, they'll be so gigantic. Why, as soon as you plant a couple of these Secret Hybrid Tomato plants, you'll have so many tomatoes that you can easily make hundred$ of dollar$ by selling them to your neighbors! But wait! There's more!!!!

You know the garbage I'm talking about. As I said earlier, most people have highly developed *B.S. meters* that detect and shut out that nonsense. When the hype marketers notice that their sales materials don't seem to be attracting many customers, what do they conclude? *Hey, we better kick up the language another notch or two!*

That's when we all get subjected to the nonsense claims of: *"Out-of-control ATMs spewing money at you,"* and *"As soon as you learn our secrets for picking up women, super-models will be all over you, shoving their room keys into your pocket."*

Yeah right. When you hype people, two bad things happen: Either they turn off completely, or they decide that they must find the flaw in your argument. In other words they start to look for *the catch*. Instead of attracting them to you, now you're repelling them because they think. *"This is way too good to be true—what can I find that makes my situation different?"* They'll conclude, *"I can't grow those monster tomato plants because I live in too cold of a climate,"* or *"Girls won't date me because it looks like all the successful guys they show in the ad are a different ethnic group."*

Differences are the last thing you want them to focus on, as you know. So what is a good marketer to do? First, you shouldn't hype with nonsense, nor do you need to. Because you did good research about a target market and its strong interests, you don't need to create interest, but just tap into it. Think of your target market like a high-pressure water line and your sales material like the faucet that opens up their attention and interest. The water will flow to you. Lousy marketers instead try to pump their general, bored market with lots of hot air.

The second thing you should do is include what's known as a *damaging admission*. Don't have your readers search for *the catch*, but hand it to them. What did I do in this very book you're holding? I said right up front that it's not a book about magic wands and pixie dust that will shower you with money. Instead, my system is a step-by-step plan using only bits of time and straightforward actions. My goal was to get you thinking, *"Okay, that doesn't sound fake but it still sounds desirable. Tell me more."* I guess the fact that you've read this far means I succeeded.

If you're selling the Schnauzer-grooming info product, your damaging admission could be that the results will not be instantaneous, but because the grooming system needs to counteract years of bad grooming practices, full results will be achieved after 2 weeks. That admission leaves plenty of room to talk about what a wonderful system it is, but now that you've given them the catch, they can relax and stop searching for one of their own.

It takes a smart and brave marketer to provide a damaging admission. The typical dull marketer thinks, *"Oh, I could never do that. First, my competition doesn't do it so I better not risk it. Second, why would I insert a negative thought in my prospects' minds? The more I hype, the better I'll sound."*

Wrong. Your competition doesn't do it because they either don't know about it or they're sheep following the crowd. Second, you're not introducing a negative thought, but instead introducing a realistic perspective that makes your reader relax and stop searching for the catch. Finally, the less you hype the better you sound and the better you sell.

 ## MISTAKE NUMBER THREE: WITH INEFFECTIVE MARKETERS, IT'S ALL ABOUT THEM AND NOT ABOUT THE CUSTOMER

This one's super easy to spot. You know you're in the clutches of one of these guys when the story they tell is all about how they started out dirt poor and made a ton of money. Now they have jets and romance and bulging bank accounts and maybe you someday can be like them!

Another way to spot this drivel is to do a quick *I/You Ratio* calculation. Take a page or two of their text and see how many times they refer to *I*, *me*, *my*, *our*, and *mine* and then compare that to how many mentions there are of *you* and *yours*. You'll usually find a ratio that's grossly out-of-whack.

These guys just don't get that people spend most of their free time thinking about their own challenges, problems, tasks, relationships, and goals. They're living their own lives and do not find the marketer's life to be that fascinating. As I said before, most people are tuned to radio station WII-fm, or *What's In It For Me*.

I'm not being critical here, because I'm often focused on myself, too. If I hear all the marketer-focused sales material I quickly turn off and gravitate instead toward the customer-focused stuff. Because most people do walk around in their own bubble of personal-focused thoughts, they love it when someone focuses on their needs for a change. And when you provide solutions to *their* problems or talk about meeting *their* needs, you'll be delighted to discover that people will be more than just receptive—they'll move heaven and earth to get what you have because it's what they have been looking for.

Gary Halbert was a brilliant legendary marketer I had the privilege of knowing who was so successful that at one time his bank opened an entire branch just for the purpose of processing all the money that was coming in for his products. Gary liked to ask audiences, "If you were opening a restaurant and I could wave a magic wand and give you one marketing advantage, what would you ask for?"

One audience member would yell out, "Give me a great location." Another said, "I want the best chef." Yet another person insisted, "I'll take the freshest and very best ingredients."

Halbert smiled. "I'll beat every single one of you with what I would wish for. Just give me a starving crowd." No wonder the guy was a genius. He focused on understanding human nature above all else.

MISTAKE NUMBER FOUR: INEFFECTIVE MARKETERS ASK YOU TO BUY TOO SOON

Why is that not surprising, given that these are the same guys who focus on themselves exclusively? Of course they ask you to buy right away because their primitive logic is: *I'm the center of the universe and I want you to buy so here it is. What are you waiting for?*

You can spot these headlines a mile away. They go something like this:

> How a Trailer-Trash Dropout Made Millions of Dollars by Discovering a Secret Technique for Forecasting Stock Market Prices. . . . And Now You Too Can Become Filthy Rich Beyond Your Wildest Dreams with My Simple, Connect-the-Dots Coaching System that Only Costs $999.99 but Will Suck Money into Your Bank Account Like a Nuclear-Powered Super-Magnet on Overload!!!!

Uh huh. And if you're such an incredible genius and rich too, then why do you need to be selling me your kit? Why aren't you in the air on your private jet heading for your private island retreat?

It's just another product of a *Me! Me! Buy My Stuff!* mentality. I'll talk more about headlines a little later, but the key thing to remember right now is that, regardless of how much you want customers to buy, the most effective sales material starts out with talking about *them*—their needs, their wants, and their desires. You'll get to the product information soon enough.

 ## MISTAKE NUMBER FIVE: INEFFECTIVE MARKETERS DO NOT INCLUDE A CALL TO ACTION AND A DEADLINE

Without both of those elements your sales material is nothing more than a chatty letter. Let's say you have done a great job explaining your product and convincing them to buy. You know how it is—we've all got a hundred things on our minds with distractions everywhere. If you just talk about your stuff and never give them a reason to act now, you'll lose a significant slice of buyers.

It's not that they don't like you. It's that they'll put your information aside and get to it sometime in the future. A smart marketer by the name of Brian Tracy says that lots of people love to go to the same vacation destination—*Someday Isle*. That's because most of their important dreams usually begin with, "Someday I'll lose weight," or "Someday I'll start that little business I've been dreaming about."

Your job is to get them to take action now, even if that action is to contact you with questions. This leads us to the next mistake.

 ## MISTAKE NUMBER SIX: INEFFECTIVE MARKETERS FURTHER ERODE TRUST BY CREATING FAKE DEADLINES

Most customers can see right through this ploy. It goes like this: "And quantities are limited, so you must order right now! In fact, there are only ~~155~~ ~~132~~ ~~97~~ ~~41~~ 17 kits left! So order yours today!"

Maybe that line is believable by the most innocent member of one of those lost tribes that's never had any contact with civilization, but no one else believes it. Let's see—you're selling an information product, which means you're either selling printed reports or electrons in the form of downloadable reports. And you're running low on them? Give me a break.

Another variation on this ploy is: "My accountant thinks I'm nuts! He says 'Boss, you're giving away the store here! We're losing money on every order at that crazy price you've set! I can only allow you to sell another seven kits at that price!'"

Right. So the boss is not only selling kits at a loss, but he's taking orders from his accountant/employee? Do you roll your eyes the way I do when someone puts this stuff out there?

Here's a great way to offer an info product with a believable reason to take action now: "I'm not going to do that fake stuff of telling you there are only 17 copies left of my Widget Guide. It's a downloadable product, after all! Only a liar would claim that he couldn't make more of them. Instead, I'll simply say this: The sooner you have my guide, the sooner your life will become easier from all the time-saving and frustration-saving techniques I have in my guide. . . ." That kind of statement only adds to your reputation and integrity.

 MISTAKE NUMBER SEVEN: INEFFECTIVE MARKETERS SPEAK TO AUDIENCES, NOT TO INDIVIDUALS

Once you are aware of this one, I guarantee that you'll see it happening everywhere. Even some otherwise very sophisticated marketers violate this subtle but important rule.

The tip-off to this rule violation is simple: The marketer uses words like: *All of you, some of you, folks, you people, many of you*, and so on. The really smart marketer speaks to one person.

What's the big deal? If people feel like they're just one of a crowd, they do not engage in the same way they will if they feel like you're talking to them one-on-one. It's just too easy to conclude, *"Oh, he's talking to a crowd but my situation's unique and different."* We know how tough that attitude is to overcome, so why make the situation worse?

It's the difference between sitting in an audience with one of those personal development guys up on stage talking about attitude, versus talking with the same guy on the phone, just the two of you. In the audience you might benefit from his speech, but on the phone you'll pay attention to the conversation.

And that's the key—one is a speech and one is a conversation. *"But how can you have a conversation in print?"* you wonder. We're having one right now! I don't know you personally but throughout this book I've worked to make it seem like we're sitting in a coffee shop talking about your successful second income.

Mark my words—If you make a little card and carry around these audience tip-offs, you'll hear them used all the time. Once you are sensitized to it, you'll automatically begin to talk more directly to individuals in print and also when you're in a group.

* * *

I suspect that you agree that the vast majority of promotions include one and usually several of these blunders. That's really good news because, just by avoiding them, you can stand head-and-shoulders above any competition in your target market.

Your customers most likely will not even realize why they like your stuff much more—they'll just know that you come across as honest, believable, and one of them. It doesn't get much better than that.

THE EIGHT *MONEY QUESTIONS*:
ANSWER THESE AND YOUR PRODUCT WILL SELL

People think in images and questions. We're constantly playing images in our minds of situations that happened to us in the past, or worse—things we're worried may happen in the future. Mixed in with all those images are many questions like: *How can I possibly get all my work done tomorrow? When is this economy going to improve? I wonder if she likes me or does she smile like that at everyone?*

In the process of buying anything we tend to ask certain questions each time. We may not actually say the words in our heads, but we mentally size up each product in just the same way that we size up a new acquaintance by intuitively sensing to ourselves the question, *"Do I like this person?"*

Therefore, whether you're writing a long sales letter or a short landing page, you should keep the following questions in mind. They not only need answering, but by answering them in the correct order you create a logical flow to your argument.

$ Money Question One: "Why Should I Stop and Listen to You?"

As we've discussed, most people lead pretty busy, distracted lives. We sort our postal mail over the trash can, not even bothering to open the obvious junk mail. We click-to-oblivion the e-mails that bleat variations of *Open up now!* and *Only 4 hours Left to Claim Your Copy!*

Almost like scanning a crowd of faces for someone we know, we make split-second judgments about what's worth reading and what's not. You have maybe a half-second or perhaps even one whole second to make your case. There are only two ways to do it effectively: First it's the "from" address in an e-mail or the return address on a physical envelope. It tells the reader whether the message is from his fiancée or a fake-filled marketer, from his boss or a bogus salesperson. We'll talk more about that in the next chapter.

The second clue is the e-mail subject line, or the first line in a Google AdWords ad, or a headline in a printed piece. If it's relevant to the reader's passion then it instantly is saved and maybe opened on the spot. If I'm a Harley motorcycle nut and that first line is about Harleys, well, that's a keeper.

If you haven't yet established a relationship with someone, then the best way of answering Money Question One is to make it clear your message is about your info product topic. Because you're not using the scattershot approach but have focused your efforts on people that care about your topic, then it will resonate with them.

Just don't do the *Buy Me!* approach with it. Instead, engage the reader in the topic, along the lines of: *Finally: A Way to Groom Your Schnauzer without Grief*, or it might be *Organic Heirloom Tomato Tips*.

You might not get the best headline from the get-go but it's worth experimenting. The goal is not to get readers to buy your stuff. The goal is to get them to stop and give you not a split-second of attention but now 10 seconds of further attention. That brings us to the next Money Question.

$ Money Question Two: "Why Should I Read the Whole Thing?"

As I said, you now maybe have 10 seconds to sell the reader not on your product but on reading the rest of the letter, postcard, or web page.

Once again, I'm going to suggest something that will totally separate you from the pack, and that is to load up your sales message with good, solid, usable information. Think about what happens when you stop, open a letter, and read it over: Within seconds you get a sense either that it's merely a sales pitch or that it's something more.

Most people like to buy stuff but they hate to be sold. They want to approach a product on their own terms because *they* want it. The pure sales letter that talks only about the promoter, then the product, and the price—well, that's a pure act of *being sold*.

That won't be you. Instead, the beginning of your sales letter can honestly say something like, "By the time you're done reading this letter, you'll know three specific techniques I've found to accelerate the composting process that's so vital when growing organic heirloom tomatoes."

What have you just done? Right up front, in the space of that 10 seconds of attention, you just sold those readers on going through the rest of your letter.

At this point, you proceed to give them three solid tips they can immediately use. When they read those, they'll think, *"Hey, that was some good stuff! I knew one of the tips already but the other two were interesting. I wonder what else this person has."*

There's a way to amplify their interest in your product, and that's by showing that you are one of them. You do this by entering the conversation already going on in their heads. For instance, if you did an info product on bikers you would know that many of them detest the government dictating that bikers wear helmets. To them the government is the enemy, so your text might say, "Are you sick and tired of being treated like a baby by a government that can't even balance its own budget?" With a statement like that, a whole lot of bikers will know you're one of them.

Here are some great ways to show you're in tune with your readers. It's all information you should have gathered in your product-research stage.

- *Describe the common enemy*—as in the biker example.
- *Graphically outline what keeps the readers up at night.* It might be insurance company paperwork, or grubs attacking their lawns, or the skyrocketing price of something.
- *Allude to what frustrates them the most.* Is it employees? Is it having to reset the Acme Mark VI Widget every time it cycles?
- *On a positive note, describe what they desire the most with this passion of theirs.* Is it to win the Westminster Dog Show? Could it be to show up the neighbor down the street with a much bigger and better tomato?
- *Use their jargon.* Most groups instantly know outsiders because they don't speak the insiders' language. In the world of competitive shotgunning, for example, the term *to go straight* has nothing to do with sexual preference. It refers to breaking 25 targets out of 25. If you said, ". . . and when you successfully shoot at 25 clay targets . . . ," you would have instantly tipped off readers that you're an outsider. If you said, ". . . and when you go straight . . . ," now you're one of them.

When you talk about their deep concerns they'll be in much more of a buying mood because you weren't jamming your product down their throats. In addition, your helpful information had the effect of automatically proving that you're different from the rest, and your readers will relax—you seem to be an authority on their favorite topic and not just some huckster.

$ **Money Question Three: "What Else Do You Have and How Will It Help Me?**

With all the preparation you've done in the preceding steps you really now have their attention—that is, unless you prematurely blow it with overt sales talk.

At this point, you should introduce all the other solutions you have. It can be as easy as saying, "If you found those three tips helpful then you'll be happy to know that there's much more where they came from. In fact, I've collected more than two dozen tips from four top professional groomers. . . ."

This is the stage where you should get highly specific about the *what* and not the *how*. In other words, you want to amplify their desire for the rest of your information by explaining all the good things they'll discover in your product.

An example of giving them the *what*—which is what you want to do—is: "I've devoted an entire chapter on how to restore your Brother CS-6000i to factory-new condition. You'll be able to follow my 14 steps in under a half hour, and you will be pleasantly surprised at how easy it was."

An example of giving them the *how*—which is NOT what you should do—is: "In Chapter 4 I'll explain that you must first take out the spindle before removing the three pins, or else you'll never get those pins back in properly."

Why is it bad to give them that detail? Because you've already established your expertise with the free and useful information you gave them. Now you're cannibal-izing some of the meat in your info product and loading more of it into the sales letter. You run the risk that they'll either be disappointed after they buy your product be-cause you already told them half the goodies in it, or they'll not buy the product because now you've answered all their questions.

By all means get detailed on the results they'll enjoy after getting your product. For instance, you can describe how they'll never have to worry about taking harsh and some-times dangerous medicines for kidney stones again. Then you can explain how they'll have three easy diet tweaks that are likely to prevent kidney stones from ever appearing again.

Remember that simply listing features is not good enough. People don't go to the hardware store to buy quarter-inch drill bits—they go to the hardware store to buy quarter inch holes. They don't care about the drill bits but recognize that the bit will get them the holes.

Therefore, really focus on those results. A handy way to do that is to continually ask yourself, *"So what?"* If I'm selling the Brother sewing machine info product, my think-ing would be:

"You'll get my complete guide to the CS-6000i . . . *(so what?)* . . . which means that you'll spend less time fid-dling with the controls . . . *(so what?)* . . . and you can use that time to make even more great clothes . . . *(so what?)* . . . which can not only save you money but will mean that you can wear the latest fashions long before they're in stores. . . ."

Do you see how repeatedly asking yourself that ques-tion results in digging deeper into the core emotions people have? It's this level of communication that makes people decide, *"I need this product."*

$ Money Question Four: "Why Is Your Solution Better than Any Other?"

You certainly don't want to get your readers this far, only to have them think, *"This is all good information, but it sounds pretty much like what Acme Industries sent me just last week, and everyone seems to buy from Acme, so maybe I do need the product but I'll play it safe and buy from Acme."*

That's the worst of both worlds for you! You did a great job of selling your prospect on your competitor's product. What you must do to counteract that risk is to craft what's known as your *unique selling proposition*, or USP. If you craft your USP correctly then there is no direct competition.

- You don't want to be just another tomato book—your guide is the first one to apply 100 percent organic methods to the growing of heirloom tomatoes.
- You're not just another dog-grooming guide—yours is the only one to focus on Schnauzers exclusively, and it includes more than two dozen ways to get knots, burrs, grease, and other nasty substances out of their fur.
- Sure the Brother CS-6000i ships with an owner's manual—your guide is the only one to combine large, clear diagrams with a video that starts with unpacking the box, all the way through sewing a dozen different stitches.

When you achieve this uniqueness, then it will be impossible to regard your product as just another commodity for which price is the only distinguishing factor. You'll stand alone.

$ Money Question Five: "Why Should I Believe Your Claims?"

Another way to state this is: *Prove it.* In the extremely over-hyped world of goods and services, words are cheap and proof is rare. Anybody can say, "I made a ton of money on this product," but very few marketers go to the trouble of backing those statements up.

I (Dave) frequently describe to live audiences recent real estate transactions I've done where I made a lot of money. I watch as a certain number of people are impressed, and then I put pictures of cashier's checks up on the screen for everyone to see. That has a far bigger effect on the audience.

That blender company, BlendTec, could have said, "Our blenders are tough and can blend just about anything." Most people would think: *Uh huh. Big deal. That's what they all say.* Instead, BlendTec showed a video of their blenders grinding up marbles, phones, and broomsticks. That's genius-level proof.

Now don't you start in with the, *"But my situation's different—I'm a beginner who's writing a simple information product."* You know how I feel about that attitude. Even first-time info marketers can add plenty of proof elements to their text. Here are several great ways.

Get Specific

People tend to believe exact numbers and dismiss round numbers as either guesses or exaggerations. Therefore, don't say, "There are tons of heirloom tomato varieties out there," but instead say, "Did you know that at last count there were 319 varieties of heirloom tomatoes?"

Likewise, if you interviewed people for your info product, say, "I spent more than 12 hours interviewing three of the top Harley dealers in the country to find out how they personally break in their new bikes. . . ." Scan through your material and, wherever you can quantify your effort or your results, do it.

Use Testimonials

This is enormously powerful, and it's called *social proof*. Ever since we roamed the savannah along with the antelope, we've been influenced by where lots of our fellow humans seem to be heading. We see it every Christmas when suddenly one toy becomes hot and huge crowds of people *absolutely need* that toy—even though they didn't even know it existed a week ago.

I'm not suggesting you try to incite riots with your info product but rather that you tell people what other people think of it, because of course people know that *you* think the world of your own product. Even before you launch your new info product, send it to a few people whom you met in your research. Have them try it out or even give it to their friends. If you don't get positive reactions then you must figure out why, or else your sales may suffer. Maybe the text is too small or instructions were confusing. If you do get a good reaction, then ask if you could quote them. Almost always they'll say, "Sure."

Here's the secret with testimonials: Don't get a *feel-good* testimonial where someone says, "Wow, I really enjoyed reading your guide. You were funny, too!" Instead, get a *results* testimonial like, "I suffered for 3 hours with trying to figure out the embroidery attachment to the CS-6000i and, after reading your guide, I had it solved in under 15 minutes." Do you see how the second one is vastly more effective?

Just make sure you don't overdo it and use testimonials that are not representative of your customers. Some really big marketers of things like weight-loss supplements regularly get into trouble with the Federal Trade Commission because they claim crazy results like, "I lost 14 pounds in a week!" You're better off talking about the nonmoney results your product or service provides—but again be sure the testimonial is specific about those results.

Quote Other Experts

If you did interview experts in the field then of course quote them. But even if you didn't interview some of the big names in your target area, you can still quote them in general.

For instance, you might have a quote from a head judge for the Westminster Dog Show about how winning is not all about genetics but instead how grooming differences are often the reason why one dog wins and another dog comes in second. You might have simply read that in a magazine. You're not implying that the judge has endorsed your product, but what you have effectively done is show that you know who's who in the field, and you've reinforced the need for your product.

Get Creative

If you sold your info product on Amazon and it's getting lots of five-star ratings, then put that in your marketing materials. If people from other countries have bought your guide—which is highly likely with Internet products— then you can say you have an *international following*, because it's true. If your product has been talked about in blogs or picked up in the press—even due to your own press release—then it's fair to say the press has taken notice of it.

You cannot overdo the number of proof elements you use in your materials. The more of them you add, the more you'll sell—it's as simple as that. As you become more experienced and your product generates lots of fans and better results, then continually review your materials and swap out the less-powerful proof elements for newer, more powerful and specific ones.

$ Money Question Six: "What's It Going to Cost Me?"

If you've ever successfully interviewed for a job, you know the pattern: At first the questions are all about your qualifications and approach to work. Then things warm up and a positive tone enters the conversation when it appears to both of you that this interview might be successful. At the point when the interviewer brings up the salary question, you know it's getting serious.

Imagine what would have happened if you shook hands, sat down, and immediately said, "So, I'm really interested to know what you're prepared to pay me." That would be a really short interview. If you've ever made that mistake you quickly learned that compensation is best discussed after the employer is interested in you.

That's why so many marketers are silly to load their headlines with hype and price. They come across like guys in a bar: "Hi baby my name's Bob and I lift weights and I'm a really cool guy and did anyone tell you how gorgeous you are well I really want to go on a date and definitely take you home tonight and maybe even marry you someday so let's dispense with the formalities and just get right down to business shall we?"

Bob gets slapped a lot. If you try this in print with your prospects, you'll get thrown into the spam bucket a lot. However, if you've methodically covered the first five Money Questions, then your readers are already thinking, *"Hey, this stuff is pretty good. I wonder what it will cost me to get it?"*

Now and only now should you talk price. Here are some guidelines on how to set and describe your price.

Know the Market

If you created your USP properly then there is no direct competitor—yours is the first and only specific product of its kind. But still, your prospects will have a rough idea of what other vaguely similar items cost. You also need to know ballpark prices from the research you did earlier. For instance, yours might be the only kidney stone remedy guide that uses techniques gathered from ancient texts across the world, but your potential buyers have in their heads that the other remedies on the market go for $20 to $40. When you set your own price, at least be aware of the magnitude of the other offerings out there.

Do Not Compete on Price

Let Wal-Mart or Amazon compete on price. If you do that you're simply turning yourself into a commodity. There's an old saying: *In the absence of value, price becomes a factor.*

You're much better off competing on value. If you can demonstrate through the quality of your argument that you're unique and you will save the reader a great deal of time and money then the price becomes secondary. If you can do what I described earlier in this chapter and appeal to their deep desires for recognition, relief from pain, or peace of mind—well, then price becomes trivial.

In Your Materials, Do Not Say Cost or Price, but Instead Say Investment

Once again, most marketers are oblivious to this distinction. Costs are things that you spend and never see again. For instance, your lunch today cost money and, even though it was necessary, it's now gone. It's the same with other necessities like your electricity bill and the price to fix that broken tooth.

Investments are different. If I invest in an education, I hope to have it pay me back over time in the form of a better job. I'll invest in IBM stock because I expect it to go up in value. Therefore, you should rid your sales material of any mention of cost or price and instead say, "Your investment in my guide is only $17," or "You can get my guide for only $69 and by this weekend you'll be on your way to having the Schnauzer of your dreams." It's a subtle distinction but lots of messages in life are subtle but clear. Send the message that their investment in your guide will come back to them in spades.

Create More than One Product Level

Even with your very first info product you should consider creating a *complete* version and a *deluxe* version. If you do, you'll find that a surprisingly large number of your sales will be for the deluxe version.

You've followed the Money Questions and fashioned a strong argument for people to get your product. Some of them will want everything you have and even then will e-mail you and ask, "What else you got for sale?" They're known as *hyperresponsives* and they will usually be your very best customers.

Besides, some people are accustomed to buying the best, whether they are box seats at the baseball game or *first class* seats on the airplane. It would be a shame not to cater to that desire.

The other great reason for offering two versions is you now have changed the decision from *Do I buy it or not?* to instead *Which one do I buy?* That's a better question for your prospects to ask, wouldn't you agree?

By the way, it's best not to call your lower-level product a *basic* version. Who wants *basic*? That implies bare-bones and maybe even incomplete. You're better off calling the lower-level offering *complete*, and then you can call the upper one *deluxe*.

You may wonder what you could possibly put in the deluxe version. That's easy. All you have to do is think about some of the materials you came across in your research and package them in the form of bonuses:

1. If you offered an audio or video in your complete version then include a *transcript* in the deluxe one.
2. Maybe you created a very *detailed spreadsheet* in the course of your research. Just pretty-up the spreadsheet and now it can be a bonus.
3. An excellent add-on for the deluxe version is what's known as *a 911 certificate*. You can print this certificate on fancy certificate-looking paper found at any office supply store and it will entitle the customer to call you for a 30-minute consultation relating to your product. This bonus alone can boost the value of your deluxe version by $100 or more.

   Remember—people think their situations are different from everyone else's. They may be happy to pay considerably more in order to have you help them with their particular issue.
4. You could create *additional video content* that only the deluxe buyers get.
5. Create a single-page, two-sided *Handy Reference Guide* that distills your entire info product into a highly usable checklist. People love these things.

   Look back in Chapter 3 where we talked about 42 different product formats. Your deluxe version could simply *include another of those product formats*. For instance the complete kit includes DVDs but the deluxe one has DVDs, plus audio and a members-only web site that is updated from time to time.

Right after talking about the investment, explain how they can get your materials: "It's easy to reserve your copy of my guide. Just go to www.HarleyTuneupSecrets.com or call 123-456-7890."

$ Money Question Seven: "What's My Risk?"

You got their attention and then gave them good solid information. You felt their pain and then provided a solution at a reasonable price. You've achieved an important milestone—now they can imagine themselves in a better place after buying your product. They want it and think they can afford it but one last defense mechanism kicks in— *What if I get it and am disappointed?*

It's a good question because we've all been in that position many times. Here's where most marketers do a poor job of reinforcing prospects right before they become customers. The blow it with all their *Return Authorization*, and their *15 percent restocking fee*, and the ever-popular: *You must return it in saleable condition with all documents and packaging intact.* That has the effect of dousing any fire of desire for the product. It gives prospects an excellent reason to think: "*Whoa, I better be right about this. Maybe I should think about it.*" That results in delay and delay is the death of a sale.

Let's contrast that typical marketer with the legendary company, L.L. Bean. What's their return policy?

Our products are guaranteed to give 100 percent satisfaction in every way. Return anything purchased from us at any time if it proves otherwise. We do not want you to have anything from L.L. Bean that is not completely satisfactory.

You can imagine a lawyer or bean-counter going nuts with such a return policy: *"Everything is guaranteed? Forever? No matter what the customer does to the merchandise? Even if it's not our fault? You gotta be outta your mind to offer that! I can tell you this for a fact—you'll be taken advantage of by crooks and will be out of business within a year!"*

That's funny. L.L. Bean was founded in 1912 and has $1.5 billion in sales.

The bad news is that some people will indeed be dishonest and will take advantage of L.L. Bean—or you—by getting good use from a product and then returning it. The good news is that the percentage is highly likely to be small compared to the much larger sales your strong guarantee will generate. In other words, your refund rate will go up but your sales and profits will go up even more, after factoring in the cost of refunds.

Also keep in mind that the book you're holding is not primarily about selling pants and gloves, but information products. In the best sense of the word your profit margin is obscene compared with L.L. Bean's. You most definitely can afford to give a powerful guarantee that sets your prospects' minds at ease. Here are other pointers for your guarantee.

Do Make Your Guarantee a Competitive Advantage
Point out how it's so much better than others. Say, "I don't play games with all that return authorization or restocking-fee nonsense. You must be delighted with the value you get

from my guide or I wouldn't feel right keeping your money. You'll get a complete and prompt refund, no questions asked."

Don't Introduce Negatives into Your Guarantee Language

Ninety-nine percent of all marketers do not understand this! They say silly things like, "If you don't find my materials helpful, then simply return them. . . ." Why introduce that negative into their minds? It only reinforces their expectation of disappointment. Here's the way the very savviest marketers phrase it: "You must be completely delighted with my Schnauzer Grooming Secrets Guide and must conclude that it was easily worth every penny of your investment, or you can return it, no questions asked." I said the same thing but I reinforced the positive future outcome, not the negative one.

Do Restate Your Benefits in the Guarantee

It can be along the lines of: "Open my kit and try all the dozens of specific techniques for saving time with your Widget. You'll wonder where this guide has been all your life and must conclude that the checklist alone is worth your entire investment, or you can return it. . . ."

Don't Go Cheap on the Length of the Guarantee

The shorter the guarantee period, the more people will write it in their calendars and count the days they have left to return it. The longer the period the more they relax and think, "Wow, that's a long time. No need to count the days." I know this is counter-intuitive and many marketers don't have the guts even to test a longer guarantee and see for themselves. Then there are the L.L. Beans of the world who have become billion-dollar companies and their guarantees are forever. If you don't want to go quite that far, you should guarantee your product for at least 90 days and preferably for 1 year. You'll thank me later.

$ Money Question Eight: "What Happens After You Have My Money?"

This is the final wrap-up to your sales material, and it's really just a summary of your offer and a forward-looking statement.

You want to leave your readers with a sense that they're at a crossroads. On the one hand, they can continue to suffer with their current problems and that's an option—or, on the other hand, they can choose to try out your guide and see for themselves how it helps them in several ways. It's their choice.

Notice how I said *try out* your guide and not *buy* your guide. I recommend that you further reduce the perceived risk by explaining that your guarantee covers their satisfaction, so in effect they're not saying *yes* to your offer—they only need to say *maybe* and see for themselves once they have it.

You can restate the benefits and how much easier their situation will be after they have your materials—indeed, how they absolutely must be delighted with them.

Remember to restate the reason to take action now rather than to wait, and then tell them again how they can get your materials.

At the very end of the letter you can also throw in another bonus tied to a reason to act now rather than later. For instance you might say:

In the course of creating this grooming secrets kit I came across more than a dozen great online and offline sources for Schnauzer products and advice. I want to reward people who know a good deal when they see it and take the simple step of trying out my guide without delay. Therefore, if you get your guide before June 1, I'll include this private list of Schnauzer resources just for you for free. But it's only available if you respond before June 1. Remember, your investment is completely guaranteed and, no matter what, you get to keep the resources list.

If you follow these Eight Money Questions, you'll make the cash register ring, as they say. You will have made a solid and compelling case for your product while enhancing your reputation for honesty and integrity.

You will also have laid the foundation for a powerful and very lucrative information products business.

As good as these sales will feel to you, there's an even better feeling in store for you—it's the continuing stream of income you'll experience when you apply what I discuss in the next chapter.

CHAPTER 7

Relationships Equal Revenues

I (Jon) was in the market a few years ago for a car. I did the research and knew exactly what I wanted. I walked into a big Honda dealership, took a test drive, and said, "I'll take it." The car was about $40,000 and I paid cash. The salesman was very nice.

That was 7 years ago and I haven't heard from him or the management since. Let's examine the situation: The dealership is still around and presumably still looking for Honda buyers. I walked in with cash and didn't require even a moment of arm-twisting. My family was with me, including three kids who someday would become drivers and need their own cars. And I might have a buddy or two who would be buying cars in the future. What's wrong with this picture?

It's the business equivalent of *Wham bam thank you ma'am*. It's the businessperson whose DNA seems to be tied to one-night stands where it's all about cruising for prospects, sweet talking, making the score, and moving onto the next target.

It's been said that *90 percent of success is showing up*. In the context of your six-figure second income, 90 percent of success is avoiding the errors I've covered in this book and then applying the simple steps I've given you.

One of the most profound of those steps is to realize that, when you make a sale to a new customer, it's not the end of a profitable transaction but the beginning of a profitable relationship. Customer bonding occurs after the first sale, not before.

I was not surprised in the least that the Honda dealership treated me that way and lost a large, continuing income stream. I expected to get perhaps a Christmas card for the first couple of years and maybe a call after another year or two, inquiring if I was in the market for a new car or if I knew of anyone who was. I suspect that you have similar low expectations for continuing contact after buying something—you think either that you'll never hear from them again, or that you'll only hear from them when they want to flog another product for you to buy.

That's what is such extremely good news for you and me. If we just do the basic, no-brainer follow-up with our customers they'll be blown away. Even more good news is you don't need that many blown-away customers to make an extremely good living. First, they're likely to buy anything you create in the future, and second, they most likely hang out with people who share the same interests. It's only natural for the conversation to shift to especially bad or good recent experiences and you will definitely fall under the latter category.

Each of your future products will require less and less effort because you'll have a battalion of loyalists doing the talking for you, kind of like walking testimonials singing your praises.

If you agree that this is a desirable business situation to be in, then you need to use e-mail to deepen those business relationships. In Chapter 4 I talked a lot about the type of commercial e-mail system you need to generate leads, and you can use that same system now to cultivate relationships with your customers.

AUTORESPONDERS VERSUS BROADCAST E-MAILS

Your e-mail system will have two capabilities. The first is often called a *broadcast*. It's pretty much like your personal e-mail account where you turn it on and send out an e-mail. The difference, as I explained earlier, is you can reliably send a broadcast e-mail to hundreds or many thousands of people without being regarded as a spammer and having your personal e-mail account shut down. Broadcast e-mails are sent on the spur of the moment to all or some of your list, depending on your goals.

Autoresponders are different. They also can be sent to some or all of your list but they are preprogrammed to go out and are triggered either by a time interval or by an action.

For instance, when you subscribe to an online service or buy a product, you'll instantly get an e-mail in your inbox with the transaction details. That's an autoresponder message, which is triggered by your subscription or purchase action.

No doubt you've signed up for some online software on a trial basis and from time to time you'll get a message telling you about a neat feature of the software or asking you to contact the company with any questions. Those autoresponder messages are triggered by time intervals. For instance, the *welcome* e-mail can be set to go out instantly upon the trial period commencing. Then another e-mail might be scheduled for 3 days into the trial period, asking, "How is it going? Have you had a chance to install it yet? Do you have any questions?" It's typical for subsequent e-mails to be spaced apart by a few days.

When someone decides to move from a trial subscription to a full subscription, that's an action that can trigger the person to be taken off the trial autoresponder series and instead moved over to the new-buyer series. Then another sequence of e-mails can start, thanking the person for buying, directing his attention to special features for new users, and so on.

Autoresponders are the bread-and-butter of the info products business. Even lousy marketers use them, though their purpose is only to send a string of *Buy Me Now! Buy Me Right Now!* messages.

Question: "But isn't e-mail on the way out, and even considered *spammy*?"

Answer: E-mail is most definitely not on the way out. Though it's true that some people use systems like Facebook to send messages to their friends, the modern world still relies heavily on e-mail. According to the *Pew Internet and American Life Project*, 90 percent of U.S. Internet users have sent or read e-mail and 57 percent do it as part of a typical day.

As for being *spammy*, that's like saying you'll never read postal mail again because you got some junk mail. Whether it's postal mail or e-mail, both channels contain both good stuff and trash. It's your responsibility to be categorized as *good stuff*. That's why I now want to give you the following:

FOUR TIPS FOR BUILDING PROFITABLE RELATIONSHIPS THROUGH E-MAIL

☑ **Tip One: Segment for Success**

Henry Ford once said about his Model T: "Any customer can have a car painted any color that he wants so long as it is black." Well, in the twenty-first century it's time to get away from the one-size-fits-all mentality, especially when it comes to your e-mail communications.

It's important to segment your list so each group gets e-mails appropriate for that group. When you begin your lead-generation activities, people signing up for your free special reports will be prospects. Those people should get an autoresponder series, which begins to cultivate a pre-purchase relationship.

For instance, you might have three or four e-mails each spaced 4 days apart, and each one addressing a frustration that organic heirloom gardeners face. You could describe the problem, offer a helpful suggestion, and then mention your info product at the end. Just like your other sales material you earn their attention by first giving them helpful information.

Once a person buys your product, you can remove her from your prospect autoresponder and now add her to the buyer list, which, as I said before, now talks about the product she just bought. That brings me to the next tip.

☑ Tip Two: Encourage Consumption

Sometimes people buy a product, get busy with other activities, and forget about the product for a while. They eventually remember that they bought it but by that point they think, *"Maybe I don't need this after all. Maybe I should just return it."* You didn't do anything wrong, but now they've mentally moved on to something else.

You can help these people by staying in their consciousness through e-mail. After your *welcome* e-mail you can then create a *quick-start* e-mail, pointing them to something easy in your product that they can apply right away. A few days later your next e-mail can check in and ask how is it going, do they have any questions, and—by the way—they really should check out page 14 of your guide because many of your customers have had success applying it with quick results.

This is a real win-win proposition because the sooner they use your product, the sooner they'll get results. You benefit because they just might become raving fans of your information and spread the word to their friends.

A great technique to use in your autoresponder series is to create a *mailbag* theme. Every so often have an e-mail with a question or two from a customer and your answer. What if you don't yet have many customers? Then make up the questions! You don't have to say they were from customers, but you just say: "You may have this question about using the CS-6000i. . . ." Either way you're delivering helpful information.

Over time you could consider segmenting your list in other ways. For instance, you may have a group of users in one part of the country and they could benefit from slightly different information from what you would send other users. The great thing about commercial e-mail systems is that they make it easy to segment your list any which way.

☑ Tip Three: Become a Welcome Guest in Their Inbox

The next time you fire up your e-mail system, I'd like you to try something interesting: Look at the most recent 10 or so e-mails and closely notice your instant reaction to the *From* name and the subject lines of each e-mail. I'm referring to the feeling you get the instant you recognize what that e-mail is about or who sent it, even before you open the e-mail.

I bet your reaction will be along the lines of this: "E-mail 1: *Ugh, the phone bill. . . .* E-mail 2: *Double Ugh, another stupid Viagra ad. . . .* E-mail 3: *Oh Frank's writing me back with an answer to my question. . . .* E-mail 4: *Oh good, a note from Phil at school about his travel plans. . . .*"

Once you scanned your e-mails, you'll typically go back over them and instantly delete the obvious garbage. You'll then attend to the e-mails that looked more urgent and maybe will delay opening the bills, and eventually you will deal with the rest.

My point is that you as a marketer want to generate the following reaction when they come across your e-mail: "*Hmmm, he's that tomato guy. I wonder what he might be discussing this time?*"

No, you're not in the true inner circle of best friends and urgent e-mails, but you're also far from being in the *Ugh* category. Instead, you'll generate a certain openness and curiosity on the part of the reader.

If you've followed my advice and have avoided all the fake hyped stuff then you're probably already a welcome e-mail in the inbox. The way to continue to be welcome is to vary your communications with a mixture of commentary, news, and product offerings.

It's fine to continue to sell people through e-mail but you definitely don't want to create the impression of: "*Not another e-mail pestering me to buy something else!*" Therefore don't be so predictable. Once in a while you should send a broadcast message to a segment of your list with pure, nonsales news: "I just came across a great piece about Schnauzers in *Show Dog* magazine. Did you see it? I didn't know this but the Dutch have developed this new flower-based shampoo for our breed that claims. . . ." You then go on to talk purely about the news article. You don't even mention your product at all but take on the characteristic of one dog lover e-mailing another about something you saw in a magazine.

It doesn't take too many of those type of e-mails to keep you in the welcome-guest category.

✓ Tip Four: Make It Two-Way Communication

Don't just talk at your audience but occasionally ask them to talk to you. This will separate you once more from most other marketers who incessantly talk at you, as if only your money counts and your opinion doesn't.

What you should do is every so often pose a question. It can be as simple as, "I'm interested to know what you consider to be the most difficult aspect of organic gardening. I live here in Massachusetts but recognize that your climate may be very different. If you could have one problem solved, what would it be? I'm not saying that I can solve it, but I'd sure like to know what's on your mind."

I can tell you from experience that you'll not hear back from some people, but others will write you a page-long response. You're the first person to ask them about what's been bugging them for years about organic gardening! Not only have you just succeeded in becoming a most-welcome guest in their inbox, but who knows—you might have the solution to their problem after all, or you could recommend another resource to them just as a friend might do. You also might get a fantastic new product idea from such responses because there could be many people with the same strong frustration as that person—until you solve it in your next info product.

Major Warning: Under No Circumstances Should You Sell Your List!

You might think that your info products are your most valuable assets, but they're not—your list is by far the most valuable asset you have as an info marketer.

Would you take your personal contact list and sell it to some no-name marketer for a few bucks? I certainly hope not, because that would harm your relationships. Your sister is likely to call you up and chew you out about all the junk mail you let loose in her inbox from that action.

It's no different with the mailing list you have carefully assembled and cultivated. If you've done it right, these people trust you about your area of expertise and maybe have even referred business your way. You should be able to get a long and substantial income stream from them over time with your own products and services.

Once you sell those names then you've lost control over how that relationship will be managed. You might try to do a sneaky sale without telling your list but is that the way you run your business? Let's put it another way: If you e-mailed your list and asked their permission to sell their names so someone else can market to them and you can make money from their names, what do you suppose they would say? If the answer is *they wouldn't like it*, then don't do it.

OTHER WAYS TO STAY CLOSE TO YOUR CUSTOMERS

As you can tell, I'm a big fan of e-mail as an inexpensive and effective way to cultivate your customer relationships. But just as I recommend that you mix up the types of e-mails you send your customers, I also suggest that you mix up the media and not rely only on e-mail.

For instance, postcards are excellent for staying in touch. Consider sending one to your customers on a quarterly basis with a helpful tip or two, along with your web address and phone number. That might be just the prompt they need to think: *"You know, I've been meaning to check out that dog lady's site for any new products she has."*

Another great vehicle is a one-page free newsletter in self-mailer format. That means you fold a piece of copier paper into thirds and attach a little tab of tape to keep it closed. One of the six panels of this tri-folded paper then becomes the side with the customer's address. It's very inexpensive to mail and gives you more room than a postcard does to communicate your message. It might be the most interesting thing your customer received in the mail that day, and it could lead to sales. Make sure that your information is not all sales-related but that some of it strengthens the bond by being good solid content.

If you don't mind picking up the phone, you can blow away some of your prospects or customers by calling them to ask their opinions. Again, it's not a sales pitch but you simply identify yourself and ask two or three preplanned questions about your info product subject. A few of them may not want to talk, and that's fine because others will be only too happy and flattered that you asked their opinion.

I know one marketer who had mixed results with a series of products he offered until he asked some of his customers to talk to him about what they really needed. The information he gained allowed him to refocus his product and earn many millions of dollars. He's that same guy I told you about earlier who had an entire bank branch devoted to processing his mail-order business.

Again, if you want to know my current recommendations for good commercial e-mail vendors, go to www.sixfigure secondincome.com and type "e-mail" in the search box.

CHAPTER 8

The Secrets to an Upward Profit Spiral

By now you know that I have no use for hype-mongers who prowl the Internet, luring people with their absurd claims of phenomenal profits that their systems will generate. Therefore, it's out-of-character for me to make the following statement, but I'll make it because it's true: There does exist a method for doubling or tripling your info product profits without spending any additional money. In fact, in some cases you can spend less and make more.

I've had to wait until this point in the book to tell you about it because the claim I just made is so outrageous that if you didn't know my philosophy you'd just dismiss me as another snake-oil salesman.

This chapter is not about snake oil at all but an amazing method for multiplying your profits called *conversion optimization*. It's one of the least-used but most-powerful ways to boost your profits.

When I say *conversion*, I'm referring to an action you want someone to take. In other words, if I'm doing lead generation then my conversion goal is signups, or getting people to give me their contact information. Once I have a list of those prospects and I'm trying to persuade them to buy my info product then *purchases* becomes my conversion goal.

Therefore, you can have different conversion goals at different points in the process. *Conversion optimization* refers to the process of maximizing those conversions.

To state it another way, let's say I have a flow of people coming to my web site and a certain number of them sign up for my special report. If I can improve what I say on the web site, then I might be able to double the number of signups even though I didn't change the amount of traffic to my site.

The same is true at the next goal—the purchase conversion. What if I could change the things I said to my prospects so that more of them bought? That would be great news.

The amazing power of conversion optimization is that it truly can multiply your profits. Think what happens when I have the same traffic as before, but I boost both the signups and then the percentage of signups that become buyers. I've now shot my profits through the roof.

But is that possible in our realistic, nonhyped world? Yes, it is. But if it's so good, then why isn't everybody doing it? Two reasons: First, many people don't know how to do it, and second, optimization involves measuring and testing, and most people are lazy. They'd rather exaggerate than measure.

It's clear that you aren't lazy or you wouldn't have read this far in the book. Therefore, you get to multiply the profits your web site will generate without spending additional money to do so.

Conversion optimization is a matter of applying three steps.

STEP ONE: INSTALL MEASURING DEVICES

Go to Google and type in *Google Analytics*. Then follow the directions to install it on your web site. It's a matter of putting a small snippet of invisible text on your web site. That text allows Google to give you an amazing amount of information on the behavior of people who come to your site. Google Analytics is a free tool, and the process of putting it on your site will take a few minutes. This tool is so powerful that I can't possibly cover all the insights it can give you about your site, so if you would like more information, go to www .sixfiguresecondincome.com and type "Analytics" into the search box.

Another tool that you should consider getting is at www .crazyegg.com. It's only a few bucks per month but it will tell you some really eye-opening things about your web site. It actually can track where all your visitors click on your site. It's almost spooky how you can peek in on how people behave when visiting your site.

STEP TWO: DETERMINE WHY NONBUYERS DON'T BUY, AND ADJUST YOUR SITE ACCORDINGLY

Conversion optimization is all about getting inside the heads of your nonbuyers. It's not uncommon to have only 5 percent, or 2 percent, or even fewer than 1 percent of visitors take the action you wish them to take—for instance to buy your info product.

What about the other 99 percent? What's up with them? Here are just a few possible reasons for them not to buy:

- They mistyped in someone else's web address, landed on your site by accident and have no interest in what you have, so when they realized they were in the wrong place they left right away.

- They did intend to come to your site but their web browser is showing a jumbled-up version of your web page, so they leave.
- They thought your site was about dog grooming in general and they don't have a Schnauzer.
- They have a Schnauzer with a particular grooming problem and you didn't mention it so they're not sure if your guide will cover that problem.
- They think your price is too high.
- They are not sure what your return policy is, and they don't want to take a chance.
- They were offended by a slang term you used about another dog breed they like.
- They in fact want to buy your guide, but they're low on cash right now.
- They tried to order from your site but got an error after entering their payment information.
- . . . And at least a couple dozen other possible reasons.

You will get some insight into these reasons if you pay close attention to the kind of e-mails you get from prospects and customers. If a person asks, "Does your guide cover such and such problem with Schnauzer grooming?" then after you reply, be sure to add that information to your web site.

For every person that asks the question there could be dozens who might have bought but they didn't take the time to ask. Scrutinize those e-mails as if you were a detective looking for clues.

Also consider installing a free tool called *Kampyle*, which you can get at www.kampyle.com. This is an instant-feedback tool that allows visitors to your web site to ask you questions from anywhere in your site. It's a way of making it as convenient as possible to hear what's on their minds. As with e-mails, pay careful attention to what they ask and the observations they make. With any group of people, some observations are more valuable than others so don't dismiss them all just because a nut case writes you from time to time.

STEP THREE: TEST EVERYTHING

You'll hear all kinds of *sure-fire rules* by marketers who swear that a certain button on their site boosted response, or how having your price end in the number *seven* will work better than anything else. Even if their rules seemed to work for them, you need to test them on your site to see if they work with your people.

You might want to test how many sales you get when you price an info product at $47 versus $37. Believe it or not, sometimes the higher price results in more sales. How nice is that! In addition to price, there are dozens of different things you can test on your site: headlines, pictures, captions beneath pictures, guarantee language, shipping charges, types of bonuses, and many others.

The first things you should test are what you discover in Step Two about what your visitors are asking you. Also, Google Analytics might be able to tell you that your visitors spent the most time on a particular page that talked about the Brother CS-6000i embroidery attachment, for instance. Could that be an area of hot interest for them? You could find out by running a test where you add a special embroidery video to your info product deluxe package and see whether it boosts sales versus not adding that bonus, or adding a different bonus.

Google has another tool that is free and that enables you to test pretty much anything you can think of on your site.

It's called the *Google Website Optimizer*. It's another small bit of invisible text or code that you add to your web pages. Then you tell Google what you want to test on the page and you prepare the different versions.

For instance, you may want to test two different headlines so you tell the *Website Optimizer* tool what wording to use for each headline version. Then the tool will show *Version A* to one visitor and *Version B* to the next visitor and will track who ended up buying. Google will even tell you when one of the variations becomes the winner.

It can be extremely profitable for you to get into the habit of constantly running one or more tests. Let's say you tested different headlines and found one that worked much better than another. Make that your new standard version, also known as the *control*, and now test something else like price, bonuses, and so on. If each test leads to a small improvement in results, the combined action of several things improving can make a very big difference.

Google Website Optimizer is similar to Google Analytics in the sense that it's an astonishingly powerful tool for increasing your profits, but it takes some effort to learn. The payoff can be tremendous and it's well worth your time to explore those tools until you're making so much dough that you can just hire a testing and tracking geek to run them all for you.

If you would like more information on Google Website Optimizer, go to www.sixfiguresecondincome.com and type "Optimizer" into the search box.

Next, let's talk about some final points you should remember as you launch your info products business.

CHAPTER 9

The "I" Factor

As odd as it may sound, if you've read just this one book you now have all the knowledge you need to be successful in an online business. You have the capacity to create inexpensive products that can send money your way, day after day, year after year.

I hope that I've swept away dozens of myths and misconceptions about making money online. You don't need more knowledge. You now have the *what* and the *why*, the *who* and the *how*, in order to make it all happen.

You only need to add the one spark that ignites the whole thing. It's the *when*. You need to start implementing *now*!

The "I" Factor is *Implementation*. It's taking action to make your dream of financial independence a reality. Thomas Edison said, "Many of life's failures are people who did not realize how close they were to success when they gave up." Edison wrote that in an age when it was necessary to work in factories and make products out of iron.

You live in an age when you can make products out of thin air with nothing more than your willingness to take action on the straightforward steps I have laid out for you.

What counts is not how fast you're moving, but whether you are in fact moving toward your destination. On the next sunny day take a moment to notice as the sun streams in a window and casts its beam on the floor. If you watch very closely you can see an almost imperceptible movement of the light as it crosses the room. That tiny progress is enough to cross the entire sky in a day.

Remember the sun and make fast progress or even just tiny progress toward your goals—but make progress. It will always be the only way to reach your worthy destination.

From time to time we have live events where like-minded people from all across the country come to roll up their sleeves and start or improve their Internet businesses with us personally. Why would you possibly need that if this book covers everything? You don't actually need it at all, but it's just a matter of how quickly you want to reach your goals, and whether you could use an extra kick in the pants to do it. Sometimes the focus of a live event is just that extra ingredient to make it all come together.

The details and dates change frequently, so if you would like more information, go to www.sixfigure secondincome.com and type "Live Event" into the search box.

INDEX

DATE			